D1078183

MANAGING THE MESSAGE

A tool kit for health service communicators

Roy Lilley and Geoffrey Bowden

Foreword by

David Brindle
Social Affairs Correspondent
The Guardian

Radcliffe Medical Press

© 2000 Roy Lilley and Geoffrey Bowden

Radcliffe Medical Press Ltd
18 Marcham Road, Abingdon, Oxon OX14 1AA

British Library Cataloguing in Publication Data

A catalogue record for this book is available from the British Library.

ISBN 1 85775 412 3

Typeset by Joshua Associates Ltd, Oxford
Printed and bound by TJ International Ltd, Padstow, Cornwall

CONTENTS

FOREWORD

The good news is that NHS communications are better than ever. The bad news is that they are still pretty awful. As a seasoned recipient of the external product, and an interested observer of the internal one, I have to say there remains much to be done. Yes, there are pockets of good practice, but they are jewels in a wasteland of unanswered telephones, unreturned messages and unfathomable management gobbledegook.

I write this as the health service emerges, bloodied and battered, from yet another supposed winter crisis. The ingredients of such ordeals may be several, but part of the problem is undoubtedly a serial failure, year after year, to control the message. Getting an organisation of close on one million people to sing from the same hymn sheet is always going to be difficult, but it helps if they all hear the same tune.

Roy Lilley and Geoffrey Bowden have some good tunes. When Roy burst upon the NHS stage as a Trust chairman in the early 1990s, he came as a breath of fresh air. Here was a Trust chairman who threw open his door, walked the job and – crikey – engaged the media on their terms. His enduring profile speaks volumes. Geoffrey, meanwhile, has been around the health scene long enough to know where the elephant traps are. He is one of a (very) few communications professionals to have won, and kept, the respect of the health hack pack.

There is much sound advice in these pages. If NHS communicators everywhere were to act on just a fraction of the authors' tips and pointers, my job would be a whole lot easier. Top of my wish list? Easy:

- Make yourself known and accessible – you will get better coverage.
- Grasp the speed at which the media move – you must be able to keep pace.
- Never, ever, tell an untruth – you will be found out.

Enjoy using this book. I look forward to getting your new, improved message.

David Brindle
Social Affairs Correspondent
The Guardian
February 2000

PREFACE

There's a story from the First World War. Some soldiers were holed up, under heavy fire and taking serious losses. Their commander decided all he could do was call for reinforcements and try to advance his way out of the mess. The action took place in the days before radio, so he was forced to despatch a runner to make his way, at great risk, to field headquarters to get help. The runner was obliged to memorise the message, since should he fall into enemy hands, a written message would give the game away. The message was: 'Send reinforcements, am going to advance'.

The runner had a very difficult time getting to HQ and was wounded by enemy fire. He was obliged to pass the message to another runner, to continue the journey. That runner was wounded and he, too, passed on the message to another runner.

Eventually the message arrived at field HQ. With his dying gasp the final runner was able to pass on the message. He said: 'Send three and fourpence, am going to a dance'.

There, in one story, is the essence of communication! In guru-speak, make sure people own the message and have a clear understanding of what the message is they want to deliver. Avoid interfaces, because when the message is passed on, it will change. Have an audit trail and keep a record of what you can. Then measure your success. Easy? Sure, so why do we get into such a mess?

Communication is easy. Kids do it all the time. Shout loud enough and they usually get what they want. Teenagers soon learn that sharing all their news with their parents is seldom a good idea. As we get older we realise tomorrow's history is today's current events.

There never has been so much 'media' around. Newspapers used to come out once a day, magazines once a week and the wireless news was broadcast at 8 am and 9 pm. Today, newspapers have up to five editions a day, radio and TV news every 15 minutes. There are local radio stations, regional radio stations, national radio stations. There is rolling news, discontinuous news and news flashes; broadsheets, tabloids and newsletters. There never has been so much media – there's a lot of it about. The questions are, is it any more accurate, is it any more interesting and is it any more worth having? The answers are probably not. But, it does mean there are many more opportunities to get your message across, many more chances for you to influence the news agenda.

Of course, communications does not start and end with the media. Communications includes how we deal with our family and friends, how we treat colleagues at work. Communications is at the very heart of human relations and organisational success.

Communications is like the red stripe running through the toothpaste tube. No matter where you squeeze the tube, you get a steady flow of red and white stripe. That's how to think of communication. Not as a department that is called in to clear up the mess when something goes wrong. Communication is an essential part of an organisation – as important as the finance department and as essential as the quality team. Good organisations get communications with their staff, their suppliers and their customers right because they take it seriously, think about how they handle it and measure it, to see how well they are doing.

In a recent poll of top industry chief executive officers, all of them emphasised the importance of communication. They spoke of managing by word of mouth. They talked about open structures and their conversations majored on building relationships. They made it clear: you don't want to wait 48 hours to find out what's going on or to be able to talk with the people who matter. They saw communication as adding to the creative energy of the organisation. Roy calls it positive gossip! It is clear that company performance and employee success hinges more and more on good communications.

As companies and organisations, either through modernisation programmes or service reconfiguration, demolish their hierarchical structures, flatter organisations will emerge. This new 'flatness' redefines the communication process. Not only does it force communication to become more immediate – everyone can talk with everyone – relationships get redefined too. We begin to realise that information is not communication and communication is the organisation.

Whether you are responsible for communications in a multinational, a huge hospital, a small community service, a start-up business, a club or hobby group, you can and you must take charge of the communications agenda. Having taken charge of it make sure you manage your messages and make them work for you.

There is a saying that originated with Marshal Maclure and was later borrowed by one of the very first doctors of media spin, the great Harvey Thomas. He says: 'If they haven't heard it, you haven't said it'. How right he is!

This book aims to take you through the who, what, where, when and how of managing your messages – and make sure they hear it.

Roy Lilley
Geoffrey Bowden
February 2000

ABOUT THE AUTHORS

Roy Lilley is a visiting fellow at the Management School, Imperial College London. He is a communicator, writer and broadcaster on health, social issues and business affairs. He has published over a dozen books on management and related topics, and this is his second book on communications.

He speaks at conferences in the UK and all over the world and is an enthusiast for radical policies and change management that addresses the real needs of patients, customers, professionals and the communities they serve.

Geoffrey Bowden has 30 years' experience in the communications industry. A former journalist, he was chairman of Westminster Public Relations before establishing Nexus Structured Communications – a consultancy specialising in the health sector.

Among the many clients he has advised are the Audit Commission, the NHS Trust Federation, the Institute of Healthcare Management (formerly the IHSM), the Health Quality Service, the National Institute for Clinical Excellence and the King's Fund. He is a frequent speaker on communications issues at conferences throughout Britain.

Outside the health sector, the clients he has advised are as diverse as, former Soviet President Mikhail Gorbachev, the governments of Jamaica, Belize and the Windward Isles, and round-the-world yachtsman Sir Robin Knox-Johnston.

ACKNOWLEDGEMENTS

This book is the distillation of experience, intellect, wit, fabulous ideas and stuff from just about everywhere. It represents data, information, gossip and intuition, and its sources are bar room conversations, presentations at conferences, newspapers, books, magazines and notes scribbled on napkins.

It is also written, in part, as an apology to all the people who have heard us speak at conferences and have been kind enough to ask for a 'copy of the slides'. If we forgot to do it – here they are!

Thank you to everyone who has played a part – you know who you are!

This book is dedicated to the army of managers, clinicians and staff, many in the public sector, who struggle to make themselves heard above the din of criticism, bad news and misinformation.

Also

For Edith, who taught me people seldom repeat gossip the way they heard it and A-TR, who does the listening for us both – RL

Gentil, for the 20 percent you already know and for the 80 percent you are yet to discover – GB

Current events are so grim that we can't decide whether to watch the six o'clock news and not be able to eat or the ten o'clock news and not be able to sleep.

MAKING THIS BOOK WORK FOR YOU

When you read a newspaper, do you start at the front page and read your way through to the sports section, or do you start at the back and work to the front? When you buy a magazine do you flip through the pages? When there is a programme on the television do you sit and watch it all the way through, or do you nip out and make a cuppa during the break?

We think you are probably a flipper and cuppa maker! Most of us are. If we're right, this book is designed for you. We want you to flip through the pages. It has not been designed to be read cover to cover, front to back. *War and Peace*, this is not! We bet you are not the type of person who has the time to sit down and read a book from cover to cover.

Good start, eh?

This book has no conventional beginning, middle or end. So just flip through the pages and get a feel for what it has to offer. Not all of it will be of interest to you – skip those bits that aren't. Pick out the sections that look like they can help. The book is designed to help you think through some of the major issues, working alone or with colleagues. Use it to brainstorm, team build, create policy and to manage your messages.

This is a **workbook**, so make it work for you. Make a coffee and have a flip around.

Welcome back!

There are a number of **Think Boxes** that are there to get *the juices flowing* and to get you thinking *outside the box*, looking at the issues from a different dimension. Some are deliberately provocative, some just for fun.

Hazard Warnings are there to point out some tricky issues or traps not to fall into.

The **Tips** are short cuts and quick fixes to get you to the answer faster.

The **Exercises** are there for you to address the issues in the context of where you work and what your task is, regardless of your profession or seniority in the organisation. Use them to develop your own thinking or for brainstorming the issues with colleagues.

There are a lot of questions and no answers. This is not a 'right' or 'wrong' book; it asks the questions in the context of the issues, in the hope that they will help you not to overlook an important topic or duck some of the tricky ones.

This is a non-threatening, environmentally friendly, non-genetically modified, irreverently written, fun-to-play-with book that tries to make managing the message easy.

Write on the pages, rip bits out, argue with it and throw it at the cat (*Just a joke, no letters from the RSPCA, please – Ed*). Use it as a workbook to prove that not everything in life has to be serious to be good. Well, that's the idea – whatderyerfink?

HOW THE MEDIA WORKS

There are TV news presenters who are paid twice as much to read the news as the Prime Minister gets for making it!

Here's the first lesson – the media is a business. Its product is news and its profits come from how it packages, presents and sells the news. News is a product with a shorter shelf life than soft cheese.

Think of a product. Any product you like – a car, a house, a pair of shoes – it doesn't matter, it's the same principle. The makers of cars, the builders of houses and the manufacturers of shoes have the same problem. Who's going to want to buy what they've got and how do they find them? In retailing guru-speak, who is the target market and how do they access them?

The market for a two-seater sports car will be different to the market for the six-seater estate car. Sure, they are both cars, you put petrol in, switch on and the wheels go round. That's where the similarity ends. Accessing the market for potential sports car drivers will probably mean finding the 30-something, young single person. The estate car market is usually to be found among family audiences or reps looking to lug samples and exhibition stands around.

The same goes for the media. The product is 'the news'; how it's packaged and sold is another dimension of the information industry. The tabloid market will write up a lead story with a screaming headline and 150 words. The broadsheet may take half a page and then go on to include comment and opinion. They are both dealing with the same story but with different target audiences in mind.

The tabloid will be thinking of a reader who has very little time, may not be comfortable with the written word and wants to cut to the action. The broadsheet will be looking for a reader who has more time and wants to weigh up the story and consider its implications in a wider context.

 **Think
Box**

How many times have you heard the expression 'today's newspaper is tomorrow's chip wrapper'. Nothing could be more true. Can you recall the items in the news 10 days ago – can you list them?

Tabloid journalism is often dismissed as junk journalism. It shouldn't be. It takes a great deal of talent to distil complex issues and present them clearly, concisely and with economy of words and space.

News is packaged and presented like any other product. If you want to manage your messages in the media you must think about how you are going to package what you want in the public domain.

 Exercise

- Pick a midweek news day and buy a selection of newspapers – tabloids and broadsheets. If you can, buy an English-language version of a foreign newspaper too.

- Make a list of all the lead stories (that's press-speak for the main story on the front page).

- Do they all go with the same story? Is there a variation? What accounts for the variation?

- Where they settle on the same story, analyse the coverage. Consider the variations in length of the coverage, does it include 'expert opinion'? What is the variation in word count? Does the fact that one paper takes longer to unfold the story mean that there is more information included? Does longer mean better? Which newspaper would better inform you and why?

Here are some pretty grizzly headlines:

Doctor refuses treatment for the old

Why does the NHS always seem to get itself into a mess with the press?

This is a real headline that had everyone jumping up and down. A spokesman for one of the help the elderly groups was interviewed on the telly denouncing the NHS and all its works and health ministers did the rounds of the TV studios trying to tell everyone there was no rationing in the NHS. Ho, ho . . .

The story behind the headline was simple enough. An 83-year-old man needed a heart transplant. The problem was, he was a lifetime smoker and if he was not to be found at home he was in the pub. Quite rightly, the doctors took the view he was unlikely to survive an operation and thought it would be too dangerous for him. It also emerged that the patient had refused to give up smoking on the grounds that it was too late to make a difference!

Here's another NHS nasty:

GP throws patient off list

The real story here is that a woman turned up at her GP's surgery and demanded to be treated with antibiotics. The GP thought it was inappropriate and refused.

The woman started to smash up the waiting room and the police were called. The GP told the woman he didn't want to offer her any more treatment!

All good clean stuff that sells newspapers!

WHAT MAKES A GOOD STORY?

There are five factors that make a good story. For a story to work it must have one of them. If you can get all five in one story you might just win the Pulitzer Prize!

Here they are:

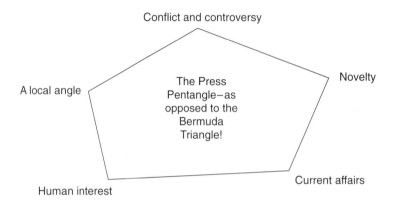

HUMAN INTEREST

This is all about 'Star's battle with breast cancer' or 'War veteran vows to keep his medals'. You know the kind of thing. It's the stuff you'd have a good gossip about if you were sitting in the pub or under the dryer at the hairdressers! It fills the pages of *Hello!* magazine.

NOVELTY

Stories like this are usually bound for the *Guinness Book of Records*. The latest wacky stunt to claim five minutes of fame. The best, and the one that was live while this book was being planned (*Planned?! – Ed*) was the story from Holland about the two million Dutch dominoes that were placed on their ends and pushed over to reveal a pretty pattern. The stunt got them into the record books and on all the prime-time news programmes across Europe, the USA and Asia. Well done!

CURRENT AFFAIRS

Current stories get pinched in what is known as the media feeding frenzy! In the same way that sharks circle and pounce on an unsuspecting swimmer, so the media comes from miles around, circles and pounces on a story.

Usually it is the newspapers that track down and reveal a story first. Other papers and news media then pick it up and develop it. Sometimes it will be a big news happening or event. The Paddington rail disaster of 1999 is a good example of how a story was developed. News of that terrible crash was phoned in to the BBC by a local resident whose flat overlooked the railway line.

The news was broken live, on air, at 8.50 am, by BBC Radio 4 *Today* presenter Sue MacGregor as she was coming to the end of the show's 3-hour daily broadcast. BBC Radio 5 Live picked it up. The news media monitor each other's broadcasts and soon the newspapers were on the scene, along with Sky TV and BBC television, quickly followed by ITN.

The rest is human tragedy and news history. The story was developed with speculation and opinion about the causes of the crash and will continue to command headlines for many months – if not years.

CONFLICT AND CONTROVERSY

Get it wrong and you can be certain to get into the press. Wars are conflict and controversy is genetically modified food. Have a fight in a cabbage patch and you can expect to be in the headlines!

Conflict can be at any level – national, local even domestic. If there is a row about it, the press will want to know about it.

A LOCAL ANGLE

This is a follow-on from the 'current' story. Journalists working on local newspapers will try and tie national news into what's happening locally. The Paddington disaster gave rise to a number of local stories in the Reading and Cheltenham areas, home to many of the commuters on the train. The local angle on crime, drugs, the impact of political decisions, the performance of schools, transport policy and house building – all national stories that can be given a local slant or spin.

 Exercise

- Analyse the content of your favourite daily newspaper. Use the Press Pentangle to classify the stories under the five main headings.

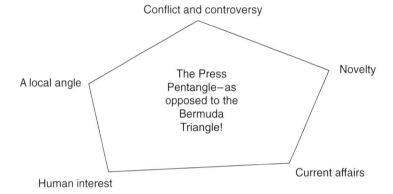

 Exercise

- Buy a copy of your local newspaper and analyse the coverage to determine the number of stories that echo national stories but have been given a local spin.

MEDIA, MEDIA, WHAT DOES IT MEAN?

In the *Concise Oxford Dictionary*, media is defined as:

> . . . *the main means of mass communication (especially newspapers and broadcasting) regarded collectively.*

It continues with a rather sniffy bit:

> *Use as a mass noun with a singular verb is common, but is generally disfavoured.*

Ooh, very bitchy!

Anyway, let's have a look at the different types of media, through which you will manage your message.

In print there are four main types:

- dailies
- weeklies
- supplements
- specialist journals, lifestyle and weekly magazines.

In the broadcast media there is (*Or should that be 'there are'? See, the dictionary's got me confused – Ed*):

* television
* radio.

AND don't forget the Internet.

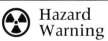 **Hazard Warning**

If you are the type of person who arrives at a dinner party and announces that you have taken delivery of a new video recorder, but it is so complicated that your children are the only people in the household who can make it work, find a quiet place and stab yourself to death. Electronic media is here to stay. If you cannot design, maintain and post your own web site, go and look for a job polishing horse brasses. The media is no place for you. Got the message!

WHO WANTS WHAT AND WHEN?

THE NUTS AND BOLTS OF THE MEDIA

You must have heard the expression *'you've got to be in it to win it'*. Well, there is a similar phrase that applies to the media. They've got to have your stuff in on time for you to be in it . . .

The media have what they call deadlines. In plain English, it means they have to have your material in time for them to consider it, edit it, and lay it on the page or include it in the programme. The deadlines are different for all types of media. One thing they all have in common is the fact that media deadlines are getting tighter. The time between receiving a story and getting it into print, or on air, is getting shorter.

This is the impact of technology. It used to take forever to lay out a newspaper; all that hot metal and whatnot. News programmes would like to have their running order fixed the day before! Today, a newspaper is set and printed in 30 minutes and broadcast media often makes changes to a programme whilst it is on air.

However, because they *can* do it that quickly does not mean to say they *like* to do it quickly. Success in the media is like success anywhere else: 10% perspiration and 90% preparation.

Your story is dead if you don't know about deadlines.

THE NATIONAL DAILY

Editorial meetings go on around the clock but they usually have a fair idea what will appear in tomorrow's paper by lunchtime the day before. Indeed, they will already have had a weekly planning meeting to forecast the news, consulted the events' diary and talked to the features people.

However, for all practical purposes the news desk of most dailies will want your news in front of them by 4 pm before the day of publication. This means your story stands a chance of being included in the first edition of the paper. If a national paper has a really good story to lead on, an exclusive or some sort of scoop, they will run a different story in their first edition. This is because all the newspapers get copies of each other's newspapers and try to pinch each other's stories, and develop them with their own spin.

So, if a newspaper has a really hot story they will hold it back until the final edition of the paper. Some national dailies will print as many as four editions of their paper overnight. If you have a knock-'em-dead, major story for a national daily you can be sure it will find its way into print provided the news editor has it by 10 pm the night before.

Holding back a story to prevent it from being copied creates its own problems. Not only is there the cost of running the presses through the night and all the distribution headaches this causes, but there is also the problem of lost revenue. If a newspaper has a really big exposé they know it will sell more papers. Holding back the story to prevent 'me-too' headlines will cost copies and income. It is a delicate balance.

DAILY REGIONAL EVENING PAPERS

Despite the fact that the UK is a fairly small country, and distribution links by rail and road are good, there is a surprisingly strong tradition for regional evening papers. Indeed, there is no national evening paper. In London, there is the *Evening Standard*; in Birmingham, the *Evening Post*; Manchester has its own paper; and nearly all the other major cities have their own evening paper.

This makes for a nice match of national issues, re-examined from the morning press and developed throughout the day with the local slant, put alongside the region's own news. The regional evening paper is a good target for a local or regional organisation to reach a wider public.

Like the national dailies, most regional evening papers will print different editions. Most of them will have an early and late edition. In London, the *Evening Standard* can print a late morning edition, a first edition, a second edition, a late edition and a final edition.

The deadlines for most of the regional evening papers is 9 am on the day of publication and noon for the later editions. However, if it is a really big story, you can expect the combination of technology and modern logistics to combine to get extra editions on to the street.

FRIDAY WEEKLY NEWSPAPERS

The weekly newspaper sector has reinvented itself in recent years. There was a time when the weeklies very nearly became extinct. They were rescued by technology and free distribution.

There are still many thriving 'paid-for' weeklies but many of them now exist as a free-to-the-reader paper, paid for by advertising. The conventional press used to turn up their noses at the free weeklies. As they saw their market disappearing, they learned to smarten up their act. The weekly local newspaper is vital for small organisations to get their message across.

What's the deadline for a weekly? If it is published on Friday (and many of them are) the editor will want most of the copy in front of him or her by noon on Wednesday. Some local weeklies do two editions, midweek and weekend. The same timescales apply.

However, many local weeklies have a neat little trick to boost circulation. They recognise that readers buy the paper for local news. Local may mean the immediate vicinity but can also mean a wider catchment area. So, they will often change the front page to reflect a local story, focusing on the area of distribution. Then they will put a different front page on the same paper being distributed in the next town. This means the deadline for the front page might be tighter and in many cases decisions about the front-page content are made the day before printing.

WEEKLY FRIDAY SPECIALIST JOURNALS

These journals, often aimed at the professions, are printed to a high standard and very fast. They make do with 2 days before publication. Simple stuff, one edition and out.

If they miss a big story they will pick it up the next week, with comment and opinion thrown in for good measure.

WEEKLY COLOUR SUPPLEMENTS

Do you remember when the average man was able to lift a Sunday paper. These days the paperboys and girls come in their Dad's car or need to use a forklift truck! There are supplements for travel, style, cooking, kids, cars and business. The published quality of some of them is unbelievably good. There was a time when we would hand over hard-earned cash for a magazine of the quality that now comes as part of a 75p newspaper.

The rise and rise of the supplement is a fascinating publishing phenomenon. As the quality improved so the advertisers saw it as a way to hit a closely defined target market. The advertising revenue from supplements is colossal.

 Think Box

If you want your message in a supplement you'd better start thinking ahead. They are planned on a yearly basis, the content is assembled on a quarterly basis and finished copy is needed for a monthly print deadline!

WHAT ABOUT SERIOUS NEWS ON THE RADIO?

Radio deadlines seem to have disappeared. They will develop a running order, based on an editorial meeting, but if a story emerges the whole lot gets shredded!

The national flagship news programme is the BBC Radio 4 *Today* programme. The sole aim of the editors of the *Today* programme is to set the news agenda for the rest of the day. They will hope to pick the story that will run through the morning news, the lunchtime news and on to the *Newsnight* running list. Now you can see why some of the presenters are such a handful! There's nothing they like better than to go off to breakfast knowing the minister of state for this or that is going to spend the rest of the day 'clarifying' something he wished he hadn't said at 6.15 am!

The *Today* programme is an around-the-clock production. When the programme goes off air the day shift takes over. A forward planning meeting then takes place at around 11.30 am. Researchers consult the diary, pick up the story lines and reports are commissioned from BBC staff reporters worldwide. The logistics are a nightmare. The availability of guests and contributors will be checked and pre-recorded inserts into the programme (called packages) will be prepared. The availability of radio cars has to be checked out and signal strength for outside broadcasts and other technical issues are considered.

A fleet of cars may be needed to bring contributors to the studio – no good hanging around for public transport at 5 am!

The Whitehall spin machine will be in full swing and bids will be put in for ministers to appear on the programme. Politicians regard the *Today* programme as THE news and current affairs programme to appear on.

Generally, the final choice of running order will be in place by the time of the 4 pm editorial meeting. Some staff will hand over to the night shift. The day's planning can be completely screwed up by a major event or a developing story – it's a stressful business and an example of teamwork at its best.

WHAT ABOUT TV?

See above! It is the same around-the-clock teamwork in action, complicated by camera run-throughs, rehearsals, make-up and visual packages (just to confuse you – they are sometimes called inserts).

TV news is as up to the minute as radio and a lot more difficult to organise. A reporter, a tape recorder and a mobile phone is one thing. A camera crew is quite another! Editorial decisions will be made throughout the day – knowing the whole programme can change at a moment's notice. The 6 pm news will try and have a good idea what its running order will look like by lunchtime, with the final editorial decisions made by mid-afternoon.

THE INTERNET

There is only one way to describe the deadline for the Internet:

NOW! We had intended to say *immediate*, but it takes too long!

If you want to see how fast a web site can be kept up to date, have a look at:

http://news.bbc.co.uk/hi/english/health/default.htm

This is the BBC news web service for people interested in health stories. They have sites for business news, local authorities and education. It is a fantastic, amazing, wonderful, truly gobsmacking service. It is updated very, very frequently. At the top of the page you will see something like:

Tuesday [today's date] Published at 14:01 GMT

That's the date and time of update – note the time 14:01 GMT – cool eh? While you are about it, have a look at:

http://www.roylilley.co.uk and http://www.nexusgroup.co.uk

If you have a web site, are responsible for a web site or are thinking about using a web site to manage your messages, cut this next bit out and pin it on the notice board, or stick it on the fridge door with one of those funny magnet things. Better still, have it tattooed on your forehead!

Having a web site says something about an organisation.

Having an out-of-date web site says everything about an organisation.

If you can't keep your site fresh and up-to-date, don't have one! Got a web site to worry about? Here are some of the ground rules:

Check!

1   Regular process for keeping it up to date.
2   Visit it regularly to make sure it works and has not been hacked into. (*What, you don't know about $DATA bug – shame on you!*)
3   Check the links work.
4   What's the content? Really, is it just junk or interesting? Ask some trusted friends/users for feedback.
5   Does it describe the organisation's aims?
6   Departmental sections (*be sure they are prepared to act on enquires and feed back – fast*).
7   What is on your site that makes people want to stay there and have a good look around?
8   Why should they want to come back?

9 If there are job vacancies on the site be sure to obey the rules on non-discrimination and equal opportunities – the law does reach as far as the Internet.

10 How long does it take to load? If there is too much on the front page folk will get fed up and move on.

11 Which search engines are you registered with and what are the search parameters? It's no good having a wonderful site if no one can find you.

12 Have visits monitored by statistics software and find who visits, when and for how long.

13 How fast can you update it? Can you access it yourself or do you have to go through a web company? Is that really, really what you want?

14 If you link to other sites, will they provide a link back to you?

15 Have a visitor's guest book and get feedback.

16 If you are providing an e-mail link make double double sure it is someone's responsibility to acknowledge receipt of the mail and follow through with follow-up.

17 System and process in place for reviewing content and a source of change material.

CAN YOU HELP DEFRAY THE COST OF A WEB SITE AND MAKE IT MORE INTERESTING FOR YOUR VISITORS?

Yup, you sure can.

For example, if you have a corporate web site that has a recruitment section, why not offer space on the site to a local estate agent – or maybe even a link to their site, if they have one? You can do a deal to get paid for every connection (*in guru-speak, called a 'click thro'*), and if a house sale is made. Well, we all know there is plenty of commission to split up.

What about solicitors, removal companies, builders and house remodellers? Oh, and curtain and soft-furnishing suppliers and garden centres and ... oh, the list goes on and on. Private schools, shops, restaurants ... finish the list. . .

Don't forget useful stuff like a link to the local authority site (that's for free!).

✔ Exercise

- List the potential connections to your site that visitors might find useful. How many of them can you make money from?

☞ Want to know who's visited your web site?

If you know more about who has visited your web site you can make sure you have the right content for them to view and that you are presenting it in such a way that they can see it at its best. Don't let the techies bamboozle you – it's easy to sort this out yourself.

One of the easiest ways to learn about the visitors to your web site is by installing a free link to someone like HitBox.com on your web pages.

You can find them at:

http://www.hitbox.com/?wmt64

Since the HitBox graphic (that's the little icon button thingy) is served by their web server, not yours, HitBox is able to count how many times your page is viewed, and offer a real-time display of this information in a password-protected area on their site.

There is no charge, since with animated links on 350 000+ web sites, HitBox gets plenty of traffic to build banner advertising revenue.

HitBox.com does more than count page views. It offers most (though not all) of the information you can learn from an analysis of your web site's traffic logs. You can find information about visitor domains, countries, number of unique visitors, the location of referring sites, search words used in search engines to find your site, common paths through your site, operating system version, browser type and version, and a whole host of other useful stuff.

It will even tell you about the configuration of your visitor's web browser information. Now that is valuable in determining how to design your site for your visitor's browser capabilities. Information includes: time zone, screen resolution size and the number of colours available on the monitor.

From a design standpoint, Roy was interested to find that less than 8% of visitors to his site had monitors configured 640 × 480 pixels, and only 10% were limited to 256 colours. For the really sad techie types he can also reveal: plug-in information for Live Audio (75%), Shockwave Flash (67%), Real Player (52%), QuickTime (49%), Adobe Acrobat (37%), and Shockwave (33%). (*Groan – Ed!*)

No need to leave the hit box on your site permanently; place HitBox on your site temporarily to collect more information, but remove it after a month or so, bringing it back every six months to learn new information about browser configurations.

Another source of design information for your corporate website is BuyStream.com:

http://www.buystream.com/?wmt64

They provide additional information you need about your visitors, including the type of information HitBox provides, plus page completion rate, connection speed (T1/LAN, ISDN, 56K modem, 28K modem, etc.) whether or not visitors accept cookies, etc.

 **Exercise**

- Managing the message has a lot to do with timing. Think about where you are likely to want to access the media, locally, regionally and nationally.

- Compile a list of deadline information for the media you are most likely to want to come into contact with.

	Name	Deadline	Publication day
Local papers			
Regional evening			
Local radio			
Local TV			
Regional magazines			

Web-site refresh (*Mmm . . . needs different headings! You're just gonna have to think!*)

KNOW THE ENEMY

There's no such thing as a typical journalist.

   Do you think of journalists as being 'all the same'? Do you think of them as the enemy? If you are to manage your message, well, there are two things you need to get your head around:

- no two journalists are the same
- the press is not the enemy.

The press have a job to do and the better you understand that job the better you will be at managing your message. You can expect the press to be probing, intrusive at times and even inquisitive. That is their rôle. Think of some of the major scandals of recent times, Watergate, cash for questions, the Jonathan Aitken versus *The Guardian* affair. All of these and many more have come into the public domain, thanks to the diligence of hard-working journalists.

> If it is your ambi-tion or your job to manage the message in your organisation, it is part of that job to get to know the press – well. Under-standing people and how they go about their job is not rocket science, it is just good press relations.

No two journalists are the same but there are a few stereotypes!

THE OLD TIMER

Been around for ages, knows the patch and the subject well – probably better than you do! How to handle them? Ask *them* for information – turn the tables. Use them as a resource. Has this or that idea been tried before? What was the outcome? Who are the people to contact? Who do you need to know?

THE AMBITIOUS YOUNG GUN

Everyone has to start somewhere. Today's ambitious young gun, working on a local paper, is tomorrow's Jeremy Paxman. Befriend the youngster, brief them, show him or her your organisation. As they grow and move on, keep in touch. Time spent with young journalists is an investment in your message.

THE WATERGATE FANATIC

It had to happen, didn't it. When the *Washington Post* did the damage to the Nixon administration they set not only a new standard in journalism, but a new fashion. Investigative journalism is now at the centre of the media industry. So, beware of the pest that sees a conspiracy behind every news release. The trick is to keep cool, be patient and explain the detail of what you are trying to do. In the longer run, getting to know their personality and building up trust is the only answer.

THE FASCINATED OBSERVER

This is the journalist who may have a background of working in the same sector over many years. An ex-something or other turned commentator and journalist – enthusiast for the topic. Easy to engage and even easier to enthuse, but not always easy to whip into action!

THE KNOW-ALL

This character is probably the fascinated observer a few years older! Corroded with years in the job and awash with cynicism – oh, poor things! They know it all, they've seen it all and they often claim to have done it all. Flatter them, keep them onside by asking for their experience.

THE BONE IDLE AND LAZY

Many is the press relations manager who prays for the lazy or bone-idle journalist. This lot are a gift! They will print your press releases, verbatim and publish your comments. They will let you do their job for them. In your quiet, private moments, pray for more lazy journalists!

 **Exercise**

- If you are currently dealing with the press, make a list of the personalities you are dealing with and develop a personal relationship strategy to get more out of the connection.

ORGANISING TO MANAGE THE MESSAGE

The difference between gossip and news is whether you hear it or tell it.

That's enough of the others – what about you?

To 'do' communications well you've got to get organised. You need to be like any other successful part of your organisation. You have got to be focused on the job, know what you want to achieve and have the processes in place to help you do it.

Here are some of the fundamentals.

WHO'S THE BOSS AROUND HERE? WHO HAS THE RESPONSIBILITY?

It is important to identify a lead person for the communications task. This is not necessarily the spokesperson. This is the person who is going to organise the function and get the administration right. Appearing on the TV or radio and being quoted in the press is fine, but there is a lot of work to do before you get that far. Building the relationship starts with knowing where to find the contacts in the first place.

Exercise

• Describe the key competencies you would expect to see in someone running
  the communications function in your organisation.

MEETING THE MEDIA

The better you know the men and women of the press the more likely you
are to be able to manage your message. The importance of getting to know
the press cannot be exaggerated. It is not a good idea to wait until you have a
story to tell – or one to deny – before you get in touch with them. Informal
briefings, off the record information, visits to organisations and insights into
what you are trying to achieve in the longer term al help the journalist to
better understand what you are all about.

 Exercise

• In the context of your organisation, make a list of the opportunities you
  could create for the press to visit and see what you do. This does not mean
  creating a media event, it means informality and not looking for an
  immediate and flattering story as your reward! This is about investing in the
  future.

DATABASES

Names, addresses, telephone numbers, copy deadlines, publication dates, technical information on printing formats – this is all the type of information you need to have at hand. When Geoffrey carries out a communications audit for an organisation, he makes a beeline for the communications database. He says he is yet to find one that is up to date.

Do you have a database? Is it up to date? Your communications database is a vital tool – don't let it get rusty. Journalists move on, editors change, media changes as technology develops a new trick. Plan to revisit the database frequently and audit it for accuracy. Be systematic and regular.

 Exercise

- Develop a communications database for your organisation. Include the details of all the local, regional and, where appropriate, the national media. You will want detailed information about the local press and probably the regional press, too. Even if you are unlikely to cross paths with the national press, having a list of phone numbers for their newsrooms is no bad thing and, for heaven's sake, don't forget e-mail addresses! Whether you are sending press releases or dealing direct with a journalist, e-mail makes it immediate and cheap too.

- If you have an existing database, audit it for accuracy. Design and put into place the processes for audit and keeping the information in the database up to date.

LOGGING ENQUIRIES AND RESPONDING

At some stage or other you are expecting the press to show an interest in you – otherwise you wouldn't have gone to the bother of getting this far with the book!

Press enquiries must be taken seriously and responded to promptly. The media have deadliness to meet. If they are determined to run a story about you or your organisation and they can't get a response from you in time to meet their deadlines, they are very likely to say: *'No one from the organisation was available for comment'*, which sounds like you were all hiding in the broom cupboard.

Log all enquiries from the press and record what you said and did or who you put them in touch with and when – and be prepared to follow the enquiry through to make sure the press have got what they wanted.

 Exercise

- Design and create a press enquiry log. What measures would you include for the purposes of audit?

CONTACT POINTS

You've had the enquiry – now what are you going to do with it?

What arrangements do you need to make to ensure there is a spokesman from your organisation available. There are some tricky decisions to be made here. Depending on the type of organisation you have, can you expect press enquiries on a regular basis and are they likely to be out of hours? Answers to this type of question will have a bearing on the arrangements you need to make.

Also, if the enquiries are likely to be of a technical nature, is one spokesperson enough? Will you need to field a range of experts? The difficulty here is that the press may not be aware of the fact that you have divided the press response duties up. You may well have decided to do it in order to give fuller and better answers. The press will just think is it a real fag to have to talk to umpteen people to get an answer or to have two or three numbers to call. If the press response duties do have to be split up, provide the press with one single contact number to initiate an enquiry and you take care of the rest internally.

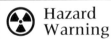 **Hazard Warning**

Listen up! Your job, as communications guru, is to give the press what they want – not what you want.

Don't expect the press to go along with a devolved response arrangement which translates into a group of people sharing a press relations responsibility. If yours is a technical organisation and the only way to get sensible comment is to involve 'experts' and that means two, three, perhaps four people who are on top of their topic, you must arrange a single point of access for the press. If yours is a regionally-based organisation and there are spokespeople from the regions, you must still have a single point of access for the press. If you look after a membership organisation that shares press responses with its members because of some unfathomable, internal democracy nonsense, you must still arrange a single point of entry for the press. They will want one number and one person to call. It is then that person's job to arrange for the journalist to be called back – **without fail** – by the appropriate person. Over time journalists may short circuit the system and learn to access individuals direct. That's OK, just make sure the individuals tell you what is going on.

Exercise

- Consider the type of press enquiries you are likely to get. Divide them into work areas or specialities. Who is the best person to deal with each of the issues? Can it be handled by a well-briefed generalist, or is it a job for an expert? Develop a policy and list of contact points.

QUICK RESPONSE TIMES

You need to move as fast as the media moves – and sometimes that means moving like greased lightning. Modern media redefines the word 'quick'. If you are in an organisation that is likely to get a call from the media, or you want to develop into an organisation that generates interest from the press, you must be organised to move fast and meet their deadlines.

 Exercise

- Consider the response time required by the media you are most likely to have to deal with. What impact does that have on your response planning? Will you need to invest in bleepers or mobile phones? Have you got a complete list of numbers and contact points, especially for out of hours?

CAN YOU DO IT?

If this is the first time you have given serious consideration to your organisation's relationship with the media, you may well be arriving at the conclusion that you don't have all the skills necessary to make a success of the job. There is no great sin in not having the skills. The sin is not doing something about it. Media training is easy to get, there are companies that will do it for you. There are courses on media management and there are evening classes you can enrol in. Even books you can buy! There is no excuse . . .

 Exercise

- List the skills needed to manage the message. Develop a skills audit to assess the training needs of your organisation's communicators.

WHO SPEAKS FOR YOU?

Who is your organisation's spokesperson? The common assumption is that it is the boss. The truth is, not many bosses are any good with the media. If a journalist puts them under pressure, or they are having to explain an organisational slip-up, they can take it all very personally and end up having a row or looking shifty!

Research into who the public trusts to deliver an honest message always seems to end up putting female newsreaders at the top of the list of the most convincing people. As a broad generalisation, women do present a more trustworthy image than men. It must have something to do with that nice Mr Freud and our mothers. Whatever, the added confidence that women give when appearing as a media spokesperson has not been lost on some organisations that have found themselves at the wrong end of the media message.

The lottery company Camelot now has a woman spokesperson, as does the organisation that speaks for the privatised utilities. One of the police services has settled on a woman spokesperson. The controversial NHS Institute that evaluates drugs in the health service has a female director of communications. They can't all be wrong.

How the spokesperson looks is as important as how they behave and what they say. Doctors, who insist on appearing on the telly talking about the shortage of cash in the health service, do themselves no favours when they insist on wearing a bow tie. You can't look humble wearing a bow tie! It looks like you spend your life at a party, or behind a glass of gin!

 Exercise

- List the attributes you would look for in selecting a spokesperson for your organisation.

Let's start making it all happen

There are days when we wished newscasters would cast for news somewhere else.

Getting positive coverage

The papers are full of bad news and all we get is lousy coverage. Did you ever hear that before? Is it possible to get good coverage all the time? No, is the answer. Not even Richard Branson manages a universally good press. However, you can increase your chances of getting positive coverage. All it takes is having a clear idea what messages you want to get across and being properly organised to do it.

First get organised

If you've flipped through the pages and started here – we have bad news. You're going to have to backtrack one section. Go back and find a page that looks like this:

SECTION 2

ORGANISING TO MANAGE THE MESSAGE

The difference between gossip and news is whether you hear it or tell it

. . . and read it!

Do all the stuff in Section 2 and you'll be on the way. You have to have a good understanding of:

* deadlines
* contact points
* logging enquires
* response times
* and someone to organise all the dull bits.

Dull it might seem, but it is the foundation part and very important.

NEXT STEP

Don't expect good coverage to appear overnight. Getting into the media is a percentage business. Your news is competing for space on the editor's desk, long before it competes for space on the news page or the programme running order.

A steady stream of well-turned-out press releases, sent on a regular basis, will position you in the mind of the news editor as an organisation with something to say. What to put in the press release?

Remember the Press Pentangle? No? Well, to save you hunting through the pages, here it is again:

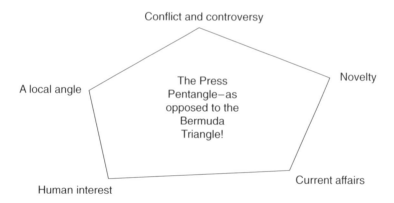

There are five headings to shape a press release around. You need at least one and any more will put you on the road to Fleet Street, or the Isle of Dogs, or wherever they print their stuff nowadays!

SET THE STRATEGY

Bet you never thought communications had to be this organised!

After you've remembered your deadlines and got your organisation organised, we need a communications strategy. What goes in one of those? Easy. . . the strategy is based around four questions:

* Who do you want to speak to?
* How are ya gonna do it?
* How often?
* And how do you know you've made a success of it?

WHO DO YOU WANT TO SPEAK TO?

In press and advertising guru-speak, who is the target audience? Is your message a general one to the great British public? In which case a newspaper is fine. Is your message aimed at a more specific group? In which case you may need to include specialist magazines and periodicals. Is the target market age-sensitive? That would push us in the direction of the printed media with an older readership. The reverse is true of youngsters.

 Exercise

- Identify the target audience for your communication. Can you fragment it into identifiable groups or are your messages broadly based and of general interest?

- List your stakeholders here:

Here are a few to get you thinking – beware it is not a comprehensive list:

1   Staff
2   Customers/patients
3   Voluntary groups
4   Suppliers
5
6
7
8   etc.

If you've not run out of space – you're not trying!

HOW ARE YA GONNA DO IT?

Having identified who you want to talk to, we need to find out what they read, listen to and watch. Not sure what to do? To give you a first clue, ask your family. The chances are you will have a broad spectrum of ages you can talk to. Next step? Ask your stakeholders, your patients, the staff, colleagues – the people you want to communicate with.

 Exercise

- Design a questionnaire for the target group you want to reach, aimed at establishing the communication influences in their lives. What they read, what they listen to, what they watch, what are their preferred methods of receiving messages.

Here are some examples:

		Who uses this?	How often?
1	Internal house magazines		
2	Internal e-mail		
3	Internet		
4	E-mail		
5	Local TV and radio		
6	Leaflets and brochures		
7	Specialist magazines		
8			
9			
10			
11			
12			
13			
14			
15	etc.		

How do they want to receive news from you? No better way than to ask.

 Exercise

- List the journalists you want to do business with. Ask them how they want to have their routine and regular contact with you.

Make a list of the possibilities:

1   Press release in the post
2   Press release by fax
3   Fax-back briefing service – call a hot line number and hit the number button for information you want, put the phone down and the briefing is automatically faxed back to the caller
4   Phone call
5   Message on voice bank
6   E-mail
7   Web site – post your news and let the journos 'pull it off'
8   Visits
9
10
11
12

HOW OFTEN?

The posh word here is *frequency*. How often should you communicate with your audience? Answer; before someone else does! The frequency plan must take into account the media that is available to you. Unless you are Railtrack, or the Prime Minister, you can't expect to be on the telly every night. However, you might stand a chance of getting into your local paper once a month. Any more frequently than that and you've probably done something horrible and you'll be looking for ways to stay out of the paper!

If you were a primary care group working in the NHS or a small business, a realistic strategy might be to aim at being in the local press once a month and the regional press once a quarter. Perhaps you might aim for a half-yearly feature in a magazine. And, if you are very bright, once in a while, you might be able to link a national happening to a local story. When the press get used to hearing from you they may come to you for comment on local, regional or national events. If it's what you want, put it in the strategy document.

If you publish an annual report, what will you have to do to bring it to the attention of the press and get some positive coverage?

 Exercise

- Design the frequency element of a strategy for your organisation. Take into account the deadlines of the media you chose. If you are going to depend on press releases, think about who will write them and how long they might take to assemble.

- List what you want to achieve:

  - once a week
  - once a month
  - once a quarter
  - once a year.

- Now develop the thinking to make it happen. Collection of material, methods of distribution and so on.

. . . AND HOW DO YOU KNOW YOU'VE MADE
A SUCCESS OF IT?

The first rule of management is to 'measure everything that is measurable'. The second rule of management is: 'everything is measurable'. Can you measure communications? Yes, of course you can. You can do crude comparisons by adding up the column inches of press you get. Buy the papers and cut out the articles about you. You can ask your stakeholders and customers if they have seen your organisation in the press.

You can ring up local journalists and editors to see if they remember reading your press releases and you can ask them why they didn't use them!

 Exercise

- Design an evaluation model for your strategy, to track your progress over a fixed period – say 6 months.

- Think about ways of benchmarking yourself against a similar organisation in the vicinity.

You could try this, but don't show the boss

Devise some press coverage headings such as: particular successes, environmental gains, management achievement, responding to needs, participation in the community and so on. Add up the monthly column centimetres of coverage in the local, national and trade press under those headings. Make a table to look like this:

Topic	National press	Column centimetres Trade press	Local press
Success	10	5	
Environment		15	
Management		5	
Responsiveness			5
Citizenship			5
			Total = 45

Now divide your monthly department cost by the total (**45**) and divide the answer by 100 (e.g. [Department cost £5000 ÷ 45] ÷ 100 = 1.1). Do the same sum next month and the month after and so. Turn the data into a graph and watch for improvements. If it gets better show your boss! If not, hide the graph and start reading the jobs section in *The Guardian!*

WHAT ELSE CAN YOU MEASURE?

You can measure the success of your communications strategy inside your organisation. Here is a draft, with some sample questions, to start the juices flowing. Develop it into a model you can use over at your place.

The idea is not just to do it once, count the numbers and put it on the shelf. The idea is to do it every 3 months (using the same measures and the same group of questions) and compare the answers and track the differences. That way you can demonstrate what a great job you are doing. Bring it out at the time of your annual appraisal and get an above-average pay rise!

COMMUNICATIONS QUESTIONNAIRE

Please take a few minutes to complete the following questionnaire about our internal communications. We will be asking you the same question in 3 months' time to see if we are improving. We promise to publish the results so that you can judge progress for yourself.

Grade all of your answers on a scale of 1 to 5, with 1 representing the poorest score and 5 the best.

'The best way for me to find out what's going on is through'

                                                             1 – 2 – 3 – 4 – 5

1 Gossip
2 House magazine
3 My manager
4 I read about it in the journals
5 The local press
6 National press
7 Local radio
8 National radio and TV

I can always rely on the accuracy of:

9   Gossip
10 House magazine
11 My manager
12 The journals
13 The local press
14 National press
15 Local radio
16 National radio and TV

continued

17 I use the internal e-mail system to pass on information
     about the company
18 I get to find out what is going on through the internal
     e-mail system
19 I read the internal house news letter/magazine from cover to cover
20 I rate the internal communications as
        (*please use the 1–5 scoring system*)

Once you have the results you can start work on improving the wobbly
bits:

• If folk find out what's happening through gossip – time to spread
  some gossip of your own, or better still, speed up your internal
  communications methods.
• If people tell you they don't trust what their managers tell them – time
  to do some work with your managers.
• If colleagues don't read in house newsletters and magazines – time to
  revamp them or dump them.
• If the people you work with first find out what's happening through
  the local press – time to find the leaker!

The next bit is even more fun! With a bit of ingenuity you can produce
a visual representation of how well you are doing, comparing your
performance every three months, quarter by quarter. A nice graph in
PowerPoint, or hand drawn, provides a very clear track of how you're
doing.
    Be sure to circulate the results and take all the credit . . .

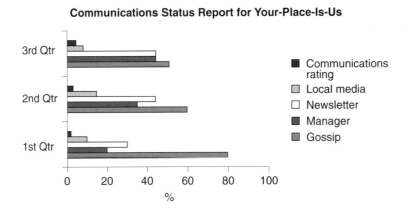

Communications Status Report for Your-Place-Is-Us

So, you should end up with a document that says something like this:

COMMUNICATIONS STRATEGY

The purpose of this document is to set out the communications strategy for the
. . . . (Organisation)

The strategy aims to underpin the organisation's commitment to transparency and openness. We aim to do this by . . . .

We have identified the key stakeholders in the strategy as:

1   Staff
2
3
4
5
6

We recognise the unique communication needs of these groups and intend to communicate with them using the following methods . . . .

We understand an important part of communication is listening and we intend to listen to these groups in the following way . . . .

To communicate with the wider community we intend to carry out a proactive press relations policy by . . . .

This will involve a regular stream of news releases about the activities of our organisation. We intend to use the following media schedule . . . .

We propose developing a professional and open relationship with the press by . . . .

We will measure the success of what we do by . . . .

We will review our strategy constantly to adapt it to the real needs of the people with whom we hope to communicate

---

Easy, eh?

THE PRESS RELEASE

At last – some fun bits!

How do you write a press release? Simple, here are the rules:

- First, stop calling them *press releases* – they are **news releases**.
- Keep it short and simple – the main message, typed, double- or one-and-a half-line-spaced on one side of a piece of A4, never more. Don't be tempted to write your life story. The aim is to give the press information, if they want any more they'll follow it up, call you and ask for more.
- Explain what's going on – aim to get the nub of the story told in the headline and the first paragraph. It would be wonderful to believe that

someone might sit down and read a story about *a popular entertainer, known for being a bit of a dare devil, who, for a practical joke, pretended to consume a pet belonging to a loyal fan.*

However,

**FREDDY STAR
ATE MY
HAMSTER**

. . . seems to work a lot better!

- At the bottom of the release have a section 'Notes for Editors'. This is the place for contact numbers, the name and title of the person who can be contacted for more details and any background information that may be needed – in which case it's OK to run into another page, but never more than one extra page.
- If you give the name and number of someone for follow-up, make sure they are available to take the calls. Having someone take a message and ring back is no good. You want a live person on the other end of the phone. If you can't provide it, think seriously about the value of sending out the release.

Do you have a tale to tell?

We've already agreed, news stories are the product that sells papers, magazines and advertising slots in the middle of the news on the telly and radio. What have you got to sell – what's your product?

It must be one of the three Ss. Is it Sexy, Serious or Sad? It has to be one of them!

Your message may be routine, but it won't routinely get in the press unless it looks as though it is *not* routine.

Here are some examples:

- The NHS hospital that let a routine, ward cleaning contract to the private sector, grabbed this headline:

HOSPITAL WINS BATTLE AGAINST FLUFF

- A company that implemented a new, but very routine, payroll system got a headline in their professional journal with:

STAFF PAID A DAY EARLIER – WITH NO MISTAKES

- A local authority even managed to get some press for their routine dustbin collection service with:

HARRY EMPTIES HIS 500,000ᵗʰ DUSTBIN

 Exercise

- Have some fun, write a headline for the most routine thing that happens over at your place.

Be sure you get the headline and the lead (sometimes called the *story intro*) the right way round.

There is a good example in the NHS. A hospital wanted to highlight the fact that modern technology means that folk who are operated on can often go home much faster. The use of day-case surgery and so-called minimally invasive techniques, means patients recover quicker and can finish recuperating at home. This is good news for patients and good news for hospitals, as they can cut the number of beds they need (as fewer patients stay overnight), cut their running costs and treat more patients.

The press department wrote a headline:

NHS beds cut by 15% after increases in day surgery.

The local newspaper headline was:

NHS BEDS CUT BY 15%

The news release should have said:

Huge increase in day surgery means 15% of long-stay beds no longer needed.

It's the way you tell 'em. Don't take on the press – take them with you . . .

LET'S WRITE A REAL PRESS RELEASE

At the time that these two great authors were struggling with a split infinitive and were writing this book (*Oh, please – Ed*), the NHS came up with their latest wheeze. The idea was to set up an august body to examine the effectiveness and cost of new drugs being offered to the NHS, to treat patients.

The group is called the National Institute for Clinical Excellence, otherwise known as NICE.

The first job that NICE did was to disappoint one of the world's largest drug manufacturers by recommending that their new treatment for flu be not routinely used in the health service. All hell broke out in the national press.

An enterprising local GP practice saw this as a great opportunity. You see, GPs are tasked with providing flu jabs for the elderly and people who are at risk from suffering debilitating side effects from the flu. Because NHS records are kept on the back of a brown paper envelope and it is impossible for most GPs to use a computer to call up the names and addresses of their patients who are most at risk, they never inoculate as many people as they should.

As the national press was full of headlines about the flu 'cure' not being available, this GP practice decided to turn a national story into a local helpline.

Here's what they wrote:

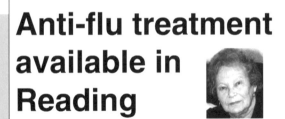

Anti-flu treatment available in Reading

Great news for Mrs Smith–she is the 100th senior citizen to receive an anti-flu jab at the Someplace Surgery in Reading.

Dr Bow-Tie said: 'This year we've gone all-out to inoculate as many people who might be at risk from the side-effects of flu as possible–prevention is better than cure'.

It's not too late, he said. If you are a pensioner or have a long-term illness you may be entitled to a free flu jab. Call 01235 45789 and ask for the Flu Nurse.

This is nearly a good job!

Let's look at the rules:

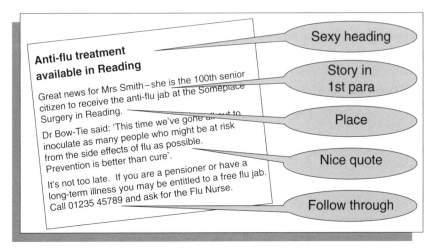

Let's look how it reads when it is tweaked a bit more:

Anti-flu treatment available in Reading

Believing that prevention is better than cure, senior citizen Mary Smith decided to become Someplace Surgery's 100th flu jab patient.

Reading GP Dr Bow-Tie said: 'This year we've gone all out to inoculate as many people, who might be at risk from the side effects of flu, as possible. Flu is not a killer but the side effects are'.

It's not too late. If you are a pensioner or have a long-term illness you may be entitled to a free flu jab. Call 01235 45789 and ask for the Flu Nurse.

This is better, the main message is *prevention is better than cure* and it is now in the story intro.

How else could it be improved? A better picture. The one of the charming elderly lady is fine – the target market exactly, but one of her having the jab would have 'said' more. Every picture tells a story!

Otherwise – well done!

IT'S ALL IN THE TIMING

Part of getting positive coverage is getting it on your terms. There are three things that will help you get the coverage you want, when you want it:

- embargoes
- briefings
- features.

Plan your news release in advance and make sure you have understood the issues about deadlines. Let's say it again. There is no point in sending a busy news desk a release for your wonderful happening, the day before it happens. You can't ring in the morning and expect a reporter to turn up that evening – they'll be attending the event of someone who is better organised than you are!

Hazard Warning

Don't plan your charity five-a-side football match the same day as the Cup Final!

Try to reach the newsroom about a week in advance and follow up with a call a day or two before the event. Try and get your event in the newsroom diary.

If you aim to work with the press and not against them, a good trick is to master the art of the embargo.

An embargoed press release is a standard press release that will have across the top of it, in nice plain letters, something like the following:

Embargoed until 12 noon GMT 15th January 2001

The idea is twofold:

1 The event is time-sensitive and to publish in advance might do some damage or dissipate the effect you want to create.
2 An embargo allows you time to 'sell' in the story and arrange more in-depth coverage such as an interview or follow-up article.

You need to be selective about the use of the embargo. A serious story, such as the need to create redundancies in an organisation, where having it appear in the media ahead of the staff being informed, demands an embargo. In which case you would want to inform the staff involved, personally, before releasing the story to the press.

Can you trust the press to respect an embargo? If you have done your job and developed a rapport with the press, the answer is probably yes. Note the answer is '*probably*' yes. Embargoed stories do get leaked. The Whitehall spin machine uses embargoed stories on a daily basis. Occasionally one or two get leaked. It's the risk you run – be aware of it, but in the vast majority of cases if the embargo is for a sensible reason, it will be respected.

BRIEFINGS

A press briefing is aimed at bringing journalists up to date with a set of events or the technical facts behind the story. Press briefings are part of the confidence-building measures you must take to build up a trust between you and the media. They have their job to do and you have yours. Together you can both do a better job.

There are four simple rules:

• get to know them
• have something to say
• make it interesting
• make it easy to understand

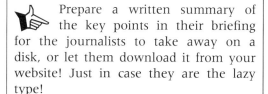
Prepare a written summary of the key points in their briefing for the journalists to take away on a disk, or let them download it from your website! Just in case they are the lazy type!

and briefings help you do all four in one go.

The briefing can involve a visit to part of your organisation or might be conducted in one room. It could be an exclusive for one publication or a general briefing. It could include a picture opportunity or provide a chance for a photographer (*a smudger, in journo-speak*), to collect some library pictures of the place and the personalities who work there (*if it involves patients don't forget to get their consent first*). Do not overlook the needs of TV camera crews when you are thinking pictures.

Be clear what the briefing is about and what you want to achieve; treat it seriously – like having a visit from a distant relative!

 Exercise

• Plan a press briefing for your organisation. What are the key issues you would want the press to understand? Write the briefing material. What picture opportunities could you provide?

FEATURES

Features should be part of your long-term press strategy document. Unless you are Richard Branson or Noel Gallagher, it's doubtful you'll have more than one feature, about you, or your place, once a year. However, if you do it right you might get one feature and derivatives of it published in more than one place. It depends how cunning you are and how well you have developed your relationships with the press.

Usually features have lots of nice pictures and focus on a particular person or activity. They are great image builders. Some magazines will be prepared to publish features that are submitted to them. They have to be well-written, balanced and technically correct. You can write your own features and mail it to several magazines and journals to see if you get any takers. Beware, they may demand exclusivity – you may face tough choices.

Perhaps an easier way is to write a short briefing note for the features editor, suggesting a topic for a feature and try to generate some interest that way. Always follow up a written submission with a polite phone call.

 Exercise

- Make a list of possible topics for features. Can you link them to national events elsewhere? Do they have a seasonal link? Consider how you would interest a features editor in your story.

IN THE PICTURE

The press talk about 'strong pictures'. What they mean is a picture that is compelling to look at and tells its own story.

If you are working at local level, don't expect the local press photographer to be too impressed with an invitation to snap his twentieth cheque presentation ceremony this week. Years ago, two smiling heads above a giant cheque was a good picture. But so, once, was a picture of Lord Kitchener and his wife. . .

Things have moved on – try and be more imaginative. Link the picture to the story. If the cheque is being presented as the result of the efforts of a charity walk, arrange for a picture of the walkers with their feet in bowls of water and the chairperson of the lucky charity, standing by with a nice dry towel. Try and be original and let the picture tell the story.

Getting press photographers to local events is notoriously difficult – so take your own pictures and attach them to your news releases.

Here are the rules:

1 Most papers will still want black and white pictures. Many publish in colour and some use digital imaging instead of standard cameras. However, keep it simple, in black and white unless you know exactly what they want instead.

Got it!

2 These days, even cheap cameras do all the work – point and click. Get one with an auto-flash.

3 Take the results to the high street and get them back pronto – we're talking press pictures not holiday snaps.

4 When you take the picture, fill the frame and get in as close as you can. The picture editor will crop the picture.

5 The picture should be 5 × 7 or bigger, black and white, and with good contrast on glossy paper.

6 Do not write on the back of the picture (it shows through on the picture editor's light box and comes out in the reproductive process).

7 Type the picture details on a separate piece of A4 paper and tape it, securely but lightly to the back of the picture.

8 If there are people in the picture name them, left to right.

9 Include a contact point for more details on the sheet of A4.

10 Cross reference both the news release and the picture in case they get separated.

THIRD-PARTY SUPPORT

This is really sneaky and works very well!

If you are intending to do a news release for the press about your latest whizzo idea, recruit a service user, prominent person or customer organisation to say they think it is a whizzo idea, too.

You can include them, with a quote from them, in your news release, or you could take them into your confidence, tell them what you are going to do in advance and get them to press release their story on the same day at the same time.

You may have to do some advance briefing and it takes some time to set up – but it's worth it. If you get the comments of the people most involved in your news release, it means no nasty press person can contact them and twist a quote.

Anyway, the lazy journos love to have the job done for them!

 Exercise
Make a list of the people, personalities and organisations that you could ask to support a press campaign. Make a database of contact points.

ACCENTUATE THE NEGATIVE — OH DEAR

What happens when it starts to go wrong?

Even in the best of well-run organisations, from time to time things are going to go wrong. It is no great sin. The sin is not knowing what to do about it. When there is a public relations problem it is seldom the communications department's fault. But, it soon is their fault if they can't dig the organisation out of the mess it's got itself into!

Here are the first four steps in dealing with the negative.

BE PREPARED

We can hear you groaning – how can you be prepared? It's easy to be wise after the event. Being prepared means recognising that even in the best of well-run organisations, sometimes things can go wrong. If your organisation works at the leading edge of something, the chances are, every once in a while things will go wrong. Pioneers get arrows in their backsides. So, being prepared means having your databases up to date and having your on-call rota for spokespeople current. Do all the administrative preparation you can. That means having identified well in advance who your core team will be and who will act as the spokesperson for your organisation (*it may not be the head honcho who may be better deployed managing the crisis, away from the pressures of having to deal with the media*). And, when you need to swing into action you don't have to worry about the wheels coming off the processes.

 **Hazard Warning**

If your organisation works at the leading edge of something, the chances are that every once in a while things will go wrong. Pioneers get arrows in their backsides.

ESTABLISH THE FACTS

What happened? What really happened? Not what somebody thinks happened. Not gossip, not opinion – just the stripped-pine-truth. You can't deal with an incident unless you are in the management loop and you know exactly what the issues are. Insist upon knowing. It may be the organisation is not entirely clear what happened, or it may not be in a position to be entirely frank about everything straight away. That's fine, you can deal with that.

But, you can't do the job unless you are in the know.

BE OPEN AND HONEST

There are two rules: never tell the press a lie and never say 'no comment!'. Difficult, eh? That's why you are the superstar dealing with all this grunge. In most cases, it is possible to steer a middle path. Everyone understands in this litigious world that we sometimes have to be careful about what we say. However, wherever you can, tell the truth about what you know. It is usually possible to construct a statement around the following framework:

- listen
- sympathise
- don't justify
- agree a course of action
- follow through.

It works like this:

We have listened to the allegations made by Mr Bloggs and are very sorry to hear he feels he has cause to complain about the way he has been treated. No matter how busy our staff may be we expect them to be courteous. We promise a full enquiry into this incident. We expect to know more by Friday morning and we will be releasing a press statement on that day.

Job done. Full of sympathy, no admission of liability, promise of enquiry. It only remains to follow through the promise and make a statement – **be sure that you do!**

BE CONSISTENT

If you have the correct process in place you will be able to deal with each incident in the same way. That way you will look professional and there will be no cause for complaint about differential treatment. By the way, if you get too many of this type of thing – sack somebody!

RADIO AND TV

TV and radio will never take the place of the newspaper – because you can't swot flies with a telly!

APPEARING ON THE BOX

More and more media means more and more opportunities for you to be a STAR!

National TV and radio, local versions, regional broadcasting, not to mention the explosion in digital channels, are all out there looking for stories – help them!

LET'S MAKE A START WITH THE RADIO

Depending on the programme deadline you can expect to hear from a researcher who will call you up out of the clear blue sky. He or she will confirm who you are and ask you your opinion about this or that. Most likely it will be a current affairs or news item. Possibly a report that's to be published, a survey or a news item where something has gone pear-shaped for some poor soul. They never ring up about good news!

If you sound like you know something and can string more than a dozen words together in a sensible way, they'll probably ask you if you are available to take part in the programme.

Here are the rules for being really, rivetingly good on the radio!

Do you know enough about the topic?

Don't go on because you are flattered to be asked. Don't go on if you've not read the report in question, are not familiar with the topic or feel it is in some way inappropriate. Say thanks for the opportunity and perhaps next time.

Establish ground rules

What type of programme is it? Do you listen to or watch the programme? Are you familiar with the way it is presented? Is it a punch up? Do you want to be part of a punch up? Does it treat the topics and the guests seriously? Can you expect to be interviewed by a journalist who did his training in the Spanish Inquisition? Who else is going to be taking part in the programme? Is there audience participation – is it a phone-in?

If you don't know what to expect – ask. It is OK to ask and the researcher for the programme should tell you. It may be they are building up what they call *'the cast list'*, this means the people who they want to take part. They will have compiled a first-choice list and hope that the people they want are available. They may not be able to tell you, exactly, who else will turn up – that happens. However, if they are at all cagey about answering, you might be better off not being available!

How will you take part?

Some radio inserts (*that's radio-pro-speak for your bit*) are done over the telephone. The technology is getting so good that, if it is a clean line, a good-quality digital phone and a sharp engineer at the studio end, it is hard to tell. Local radio uses telephone inserts all the time, national radio prefers the real thing.

If you agree to be interviewed over the phone, from your office or home, pick a quiet room, hang a sign on the door that says you are on the radio and not to be disturbed. Bribe the children, put the dog in the garden and turn the radio off. Cross your fingers that some berk won't come rushing in and say: 'Is that right; you're on the radio?'.

The station might decide to interview you from a radio car. They'll park a small van, with a huge aerial, outside your office, or front door – the neighbours will love that! Or, they might send you off to what is called an ISDN remote studio. These are self-operated studios dotted around the place. The BBC seems to have them in the most unlikely places. They are usually about the size of a broom cupboard! You turn up, someone lets you in (*access to Geoffrey's local BBC station in Brighton is controlled by a buzzer on the door from Crawley 20 miles away!*) and you follow a set of printed instructions, press some buttons and bingo, you're on the air!

They might offer to send a car for you and take you to the studio. This is the best option. Never offer to drive yourself in, unless you really have to. This is not about saving petrol money it's about risk limitation! Time, tide, a good cup of tea and radio schedules wait for no one! If you are on the 2 pm show, 2.15 pm won't do. Punctuality is everything. If you go in your car and you are stuck in traffic, break down or get lost, it's down to you and the producer, before having a heart attack, will make a note never to use you again.

On the other hand, if the studio car packs up or there is a problem, it's not down to you. The worst that can happen is that the driver will get the sack and the producer will be very nice to you, full of apologies and will certainly want to make it up to you by using you next time.

Additionally, the time spent in the car can be used to collect your thoughts and think about the issues, and you will arrive composed and ready to knock 'em dead.

Avoid jargon

Are you an expert? They'll have you on air because they think you are. The trouble with experts is they often have a language all of their own. Jargon, trade jargon, expert speak, technical points – everyday language to you. Most likely techno-jargon will drive half the listeners barmy and the other half looking for the off switch. If your world does use a foreign language, try and translate for the benefit of the listeners! Think about what you are going to say.

If you do find yourself slipping into jargon the interviewer will probably ask you to explain what it means. A neat way of correcting yourself might be to say: 'In the *organisation* we use the expression, blah, blah, and by that we mean . . .'. See, off the hook, without sounding patronising. Easy!

What are you going to say?

OK, so you're an expert and you're full of interesting knowledge about the topic. Stop, think. Think about being at one of those parties when someone says to you: 'What do you do, then?' Groan! Can you tell them, in words of one syllable? There will be a lot of people listening who will know *'of'* the topic, but they won't know *'about'* the topic. That's why they are listening to you. So, first message keep it simple – even if you are on the air with another expert and you are arguing the toss about nuclear fission. Keep it simple, please, we might be listening . . . .

Next, have a clear idea about what you want to say. What is the key message you want to get over? What is the statement you must make at all costs? Most messages can be broken down into three key points – the communication triangle:

Where you are now

What you're going to do   Where you want to be

This is the path to the so-called 'sound bite' – a few, well-chosen words that stick in the memory and fix the issue in the mind.

The best, recent, example of this was during the Kosovo war in the former Yugoslavia. The Balkan history is labyrinthine. The complexities of the communities, their status, and the trials and tribulations is a twisting path, impossible for the average person to take in. The NATO allies were under pressure for accidental, so-called, collateral damage; armchair generals were waging war in the letters column of *The Times* newspaper and the public was starting to lose patience and confidence.

Enter Alistair Campbell the Number 10 press officer. The next thing we hear the Prime Minister saying is:

Our objective is clear; Milosovic's troops out, our troops in, refugees go home.

Easy! Three points of the triangle equals nice, concise sound bite!

 Exercise

Using the three-point principle, express, in 'sound-bite' fashion, the objectives of your organisation. Too difficult? No! The NHS's new outfit charged with the complex task of evaluating medicines and treatments, called NICE, was faced with a similar problem. How could they boil down into a sound bite the intricate tasks they are faced with. They did it:

We will find out what treatments are available, see if they work and if they do, try and ensure we all have access to them . . .

OK, now it's your turn:

1
2
3

What else about what to say?

The average radio interview lasts about 3 minutes and 30 seconds. To make the best use of the time, prepare to work in three elements. The first used to get your message across, the second to deal with questions and develop the answers, and the third to sum up and leave the lasting impression you want – keep an eye on the time and aim to have the last word!

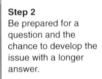

Step 1
Respond to the interviewer's first question, or introduction with a short version of your full answer. Use the three-point triangle to prepare for this. Make this the key point you want to deliver.

Step 2
Be prepared for a question and the chance to develop the issue with a longer answer.

Step 3
Keep an eye on the time and towards the end of the interview use a summary, around the three-step approach, to conclude.

How does this work in practice? Let's eaves drop on an interview . . .

'So Mr Smooth-Talk, you can't expect us to believe you can give people a decent service for this kind of money, do you?'

'We are a new and small organisation and we are using our size and position in a niche market to reduce our overheads to a minimum to give extraordinary value for money.'

At this point the interviewer will want to talk about the 'newness' of the organisation, seek reassurances you're not here today and gone tomorrow and so on. As the interview draws to a close, expect the interviewee to wrap up with:

'Being new gives us a fresh start and being small makes us much more efficient, we look forward to providing excellent value for money for many years to come . . . .'

Yup, this is a simple example but it gives you the idea of the rhythm of an interview and what to aim for.

The real message here is **practice**. There are few naturals in broadcasting, it takes hard work and practice. If you are going to be interviewed, have a work colleague run through the likely questions and rehearse your answers. Even if the interviewer does not oblige with the exact questions you have been practising, you will have some idea of what to say lurking in the front part of your enormous brain-box!

THE SECRET OF SUCCESS? THE THREE PS

Be **Prepared**. (Know your stuff. Don't do the interview if you don't!)
Practice. (Run through with a friend or colleague, sort out the triangle.)
Don't **Panic**!

Don't **Panic**? Yup, here are the dos and don'ts:

- Don't get angry, even if the interviewer is a pig! Stay calm and never walk out of a studio.
- Don't worry if you don't get asked about the bit you were desperate to get across. Use a broadcaster's trick called the bridge. Here's how it works.

Let's imagine you want to talk about a new service and the interviewer wants to talk about an older service that was not too hot. He says: 'There have been a lot of complaints about what you were doing, several of the people rang this radio station to complain.'

You say: *'I'm sorry to hear that. Our new service gives us the opportunity to learn those lessons and develop a whole new approach that will . . .'.*

See, you are back in charge and are following your agenda, not the interviewer's. Politicians are really good at 'the bridge'. Listen out for bridges next time you hear an experienced broadcaster at work.

Don't worry if you get hit between the eyes with a provocative question that makes a totally false allegation about your organisation.

If this happens, stamp on it straight away. Kill it stone dead. Say something like: *'No that's not the case . . .'* and without stopping for breath get on to the positive part of your agenda. Don't pause as the interviewer might get back in.

For example: 'Aren't you all about rationing what you do?' *'Absolutely not, rationing plays no part in what we do. We are about making sure we get the best value for money, all the time, for everyone.'*

Too easy, isn't it!

If you are on air with another person, arguing the other part of the case, or taking part in a phone-in and the same sort of thing happens, what to do? You must avoid giving a response that might provoke the others into saying: 'Are you calling me a liar?'

Try saying: *'I'm sorry you see it that way, but it really isn't the case.* Or: *'It wouldn't be fair to say that. The truth is. . .'.* Perhaps try: *'Well, my experience is quite different, the way I see it, is . . .'.*

- Do try and keep your voice level, steady and interesting. Some broad-casters have started wearing a headset; microphone and earphones combined enabling them to stand up while they are on air. Music presenters do it quite a lot. The theory is, and it is probably true, you can 'hear' body language. The voice is more animated and interesting if the body is moving. Roy says never make an important phone call sitting down. This is good advice. If you are doing an interview over the phone, be sure to stand up!
- Don't fidget! You can hear rustling papers on air. If you are a Biro-clicker, put your Biro in your pocket and make sure your pager and mobile phone are turned off!
- Do use notes if you need to, but don't read them out. Use a bigger-than-average, clear typeface – it makes them easier to glance at, if you are in a nervous panic!
- Do enjoy the experience. You'll be nervous, everyone is, even the sea-soned professionals. The day you don't get a buzz from it is the day to stop doing it. Channel your nervous energy into your performance and think of working on the radio as having a conversation with a long-lost friend. Even if the interviewer is aggressive and rotten phone-in calls are coming thick and fast, the radio station will want you to do well – they want good programmes.
- Do realise that the journalist who asks you challenging questions is your best friend, because it allows you to present your side of the story.

 Exercise

- Make a list of the things that you know about, well enough, to be on the radio.

    If the answer doesn't add up to your job description — you're in trouble!

Here's something that is so important it is a hazard warning, a tip, a think box and an exercise, all rolled into one

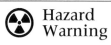 **Hazard**
Warning

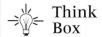 **Think**
Box

 Exercise

- What are the questions you don't want to answer? There will be something about your plan, project, press release, organisation, life or parrot's cage that you don't want to answer questions about.

  Make a list of them here:

- Now decide how you are going to answer them! You can bet your last cough sweet it is the very question some charming journalist will want to ask you all about. Because you don't want to answer it doesn't mean they don't want to ask it. If there is a flaw in you or what you are doing, start by being honest with yourself about it. Then develop the answers you want to give and bridge out of it. What's 'bridging'? Well it's here somewhere. (*Try a couple of pages back.*)

 Take a break, think hard . . .

GOING ON THE TELLY?

Great, just when you had the perfect face for radio!

Did you hear about the person who appeared on TV? They had so little personality, they came out in black and white!

TIPS ON BEING ON TV

Easy stuff, just read everything in the previous section about being on the radio – it's just the same.

 Make a cup of coffee and read the radio section, then come back and we'll tell you the extra bits you need to know.

Ready for this? OK . . .

The extra bits you need to know are really about personal presentation and how you look.

- Sit up straight, sometimes difficult on sets that use sofas. Ladies think about skirt length.
- Be sure to pull your jacket down at the back, otherwise you'll look like the hunchback of Notre-Telly.
- Try to avoid wearing patterns that 'flare'. Prince of Wales checks are no good for telly, some tweeds make the cameras go boss-eyed.
- Plain dark colours for men and pastels for women are best.
- A pastel blue shirt is better than a white one.
- Daft ties look even daffier on the telly and you can't look humble wearing a bow tie.
- Dangly earrings make women look like Mystic Meg or Bet Lynch and are distracting to the viewer.
- Men's legs look better with long socks – a gap of white skin between the top of a short sock and a trouser bottom isn't sexy.
- Ostentatious jewellery makes men look like Sid Rip-Off and women look like Gladys Anybody's.
- Using notes is best avoided – makes you look uncertain and furtive; making notes to respond to a question is OK – just.

LOOKING GOOD AT LOOKING GOOD

Where to look, what to look at and how to look even better

- Always look at the interviewer or other guests *not* the camera.
- If you are on your own, in a remote studio, doing (in telly-speak) a *down-the-line*, look directly into the camera at all times. Looking above or to the side makes you look like living proof that care in the community doesn't work.
- If there is a feed from the studio back to you, and you can see pictures of the programme as it is broadcast, hang your raincoat over it, prop a newspaper against it or turn it around. Otherwise you'll be tempted to speak and look at your beautiful self at the same time and you'll look to the viewers like you are a cupcake short of a tea party.
- If you are in a remote place contributing to an in-studio discussion, don't relax for a moment, you won't be able to tell when the director will have the camera on you. Even when the discussion comes to a close, keep looking into the camera until a technician or a voice tells you: 'Thanks, that's it, we're off-air'.

> ☢ **Hazard Warning**
> When you are in a studio the sound technician will clip a microphone to you. Let them put it on you and don't move until *they* take it off. Sit tight until they show you where to go. Otherwise you run the risk of standing up, pulling the microphone cable across the studio floor, tipping over a camera, starting a fire and burning the studio down. The chances are, you won't get invited back!

- Never, never, never drink alcohol before broadcasting on radio or TV. TV studios, in particular, have 'green', or hospitality, rooms that resemble off-licences. Stay off the booze until after the show.
- Stick to soft drinks, preferably still water that is not chilled or too cold. Cold drinks and very hot drinks do something to the vocal chords (tighten them up) and your voice will be funny and you run the risk of a coughing fit.
- TV studios are cold places, until the lights come on and then they warm up a bit. The combination of nervousness, a cold studio and thin, summer clothes can make some folk feel very uncomfortable.
- Get your eyes used to the bright studio lights – look up towards them (not at them, or all you will see, for a week, is a yellow blob), and avoid a screwed-up eye look, on air.

Make-up?

Most TV studios will offer you make-up – should you accept it?

The answer is: **YES!**

Got the message? Women don't seem to have a problem with this; it's the men who are a pest and it is the men who most need make-up. Make-up artists are highly skilled, professional folk and their sole aim in life is to make you look better than you do! Impossible – wanna bet!

Most busy people are up at the crack of dawn and off to work. They will get a call from a TV studio to take part in a programme that goes out after 6 pm or later. By the time we get to the studio we all look like death. Men will have a five o'clock shadow and the ladies – well, they know!

The make-up artist will lose the bags under the eyes, the five o'clock shadow and the 'I've been working like a slave all day' pallor. Not only that, unmade-up, sweaty faces pick up the lights and shine. Bald heads look like lighthouses and noses flash like beacons on a pedestrian crossing.

Women will probably be asked if they'd like to use their own make-up. If you are a woman who does not normally wear make-up, all the same rules apply. Think of it less as a vanity issue and more as a technical issue.

Some men regard make up as 'suspect'. Again the message is *Think of it less as a vanity issue and more as a technical issue.*

 Think Box

There is a famous *make-up* story about a televised debate between Richard Nixon and the presidential hopeful Jack Kennedy. The programme went out live, mid-evening. Kennedy accepted make-up, looked young and cool. Nixon declined and looked sweaty and tired.

The rest is history . . .

WHAT HAPPENS WHEN IT ALL GOES WRONG?

If you've got someone who's good in a crisis, get rid of them. Otherwise, you'll always have a crisis!

CRISIS PRESS MANAGEMENT

No, we don't like the word crisis. Crisis means catastrophe, emergency, disaster and implies the organisation is not ready. It gives the impression the place is in turmoil and caught unawares – not the notion that professional message managers and communicators want to create.

We prefer . . .

UNPLANNED INCIDENT MEDIA MANAGEMENT

This phrase acknowledges the fact that not everything can be anticipated, but we can plan to deal with the unexpected. It's a mind-set 'thing'. So, if you've got your mind set in the right groove, we will proceed!

EXPECT THE UNEXPECTED

There are different types of unplanned incidents that can be typified as a type of crises.

Self-generated

Here are some examples from the NHS. We could just as easily take examples from the rail industry, nuclear fuels or a car production facility:

- Beverley Allitt – the nurse who was found guilty of killing her patients.
- Kent & Canterbury smear tests – so many of them turned out to be inaccurate that women were put through the anxiety of retesting, and some of them were found to be positive.
- Bristol heart doctors – paediatric surgeons working at the leading edge of heart surgery, who had a very high death rate among their tiny patients.
- Breast screening failures – seemingly, at one time, endemic in the system.
- Newborn babies stolen – hospitals have since spent thousands of pounds turning maternity units into fortresses.
- Needles in babies – inexplicably, surgical debris and needles were found to be still inside patients after clinical and surgical procedures.

Externally generated

Some general disasters from recent news:

- Dr Harold Shipman.
- Paddington rail disaster.
- Jnebworth air crash.
- IRA bombing of Deal Barracks.
- King's Cross underground fire.

But wait . . .

Were any of them brainstormed as a potential for disaster? Could the messages have been managed better if communications had been an integral part of the disaster planning process?

Are there any common factors?

GETTING IT RIGHT ABOUT GETTING IT WRONG

If something is *done*, it carries the risk of being done wrong, badly or not at all. It is possible to analyse the risks involved and manage them. In management guru-speak: risk management.

There are four principles that are used in risk management planning:

- Identify the risk – *figure out what is likely to foul up.*
- Analyse the risk – *think about what the chances are of it happening, its impact and whether it matters.*
- Controlling the risk – *is there anything you can do about it?*
- Costing the risk – *not just in money terms (but that too), what is the cost of getting it right against the cost of getting it wrong?*

 Make a cup of coffee and think about the four factors . . .

The four factors are right out of the risk management textbook (*Actually Roy is too modest to tell you it is his book, published by Radcliffe – Ed*) and are intended to be used as a guiding principle for line managers, risk insurers and project managers.

Can't they be used to assess the likely communications risks and responses in your organisation?

 Exercise

- They say all management is easy, with the benefit of hindsight. True enough! But, an unusual amount of common sense is sometimes called wisdom. Evaluate the disaster examples on the previous pages. Place them against the four principles of risk management and decide how many of them might have been foreseen.

Exercise

Think about where you work. Draw up a list of likely risks that could turn into an unplanned event or crisis. Assess the communications implications under the four headings.

THE PRICE OF GETTING IT WRONG IS THE COST OF GETTING IT RIGHT . . .

What is at stake when disaster strikes?

Everything

. . . that's all – just everything.

The most precious asset your organisation has is its reputation. The people most likely to be able to resuscitate a flagging reputation are the communications group. Go back to the beginning of the book – remember the bit about the stripe in the toothpaste? If communications is an integral part of everything you do, it will make managing a public and press relations mess a whole lot easier.

WHAT ELSE IS AT RISK?

- Staff morale – there is evidence to show that after a major mess up, a significant percentage of middle-ranking staff jump ship to other jobs. This is not good news, as they take with them not just their skills, but their experience, perceptions and gossip. The damage to an organisation can rustle through the undergrowth for years.

- Individual careers – not just for the people most closely involved. It's that perception thing again. Put another way, mud sticks. If an employee, however good, works in an organisation that has a big foul up, the perception can be: the organisation is a mess and so is everyone that works there. The Bristol baby doctor enquiry, ongoing as we go to press, suggests that it was not just the surgeons who were to blame but it was the whole organisation that had failed. A few individuals won't want to overemphasise their time at Bristol on their CVs in the future, we suspect.

- The confidence of the people who use the services – patients, customers, suppliers, associates, voluntary supporters all take a knock. In the public sector, vulnerable and at-risk people may shy away from a service with a poor reputation and thereby put themselves at greater risk. In the NHS, there is some evidence to show that following the screening scandals some women were less willing to come forward for screening – on the grounds that it was an unreliable service, so why bother. This could lead to personal disasters.

- Relationships with key partner organisations – suppliers, trade organisations and, in the public services, other public services such as police, fire service, social services, Community Health Councils, other trusts, health authorities.

- Relationships with local and national politicians on whom you may rely for support in the recovery period or in the future.

 Exercise

- Who and what are the key relationships for your organisation? Make a list of them. Now evaluate the list in terms of how solid the relationships are. Rate them on a scale of one to ten. Would they stand up if you hit a really bad public relations problem?

- What can you do to make the relationships 'weatherproof'?

BE LIKE THE BOY SCOUTS - BE PREPARED

If you live in the real world you will realise that no one and no organisation is immune from public relations and communications problems. Do the risk analysis. Here are the four points again:

- Identify the risk – *figure out what is likely to foul up.*
- Analyse the risk – *think about what the chances are of it happening, its impact and whether it matters.*
- Controlling the risk – *is there anything you can do about it?*
- Costing the risk – *not just in money terms (but that too), what is the cost of getting it right against the cost of getting it wrong?*

This is an exercise you need to do with colleagues. Brainstorm the issues. Make a list of what might go wrong, however trivial and however unlikely – this is the bit that needs to have some ownership from everyone involved. Then start to develop a plan.

Don't underestimate what could happen.

When the senior manager of a well-known company was investigated for fraud, the switchboard was jammed for three days. Reporters sneaked into the factory disguised as workers. A TV company paid £1000 a day to the resident of a flat that overlooked the car park and entrance to the factory. Legitimate visitors were pestered for their views as they ran the gauntlet of journalists waiting outside the gates.

The manager's house was put under siege, the garden tramped and the neighbours bribed for photographs and anecdotes about the man and his family. The school his daughter attended was the subject of similar tactics. The university at which the manager had been a student was approached for stories and pictures.

The manager's colleagues arrived at their homes to find journalists waiting to quiz them and a secretary who had once worked for the man was telephoned at 3 am and asked to appear on breakfast TV.

Could all this have been avoided? Probably not, but with a bit of forethought and planning it could have been made a lot easier.

LET'S MAKE A START

Here's a checklist of some of the things to consider.

First

Got it!

- Appoint a nucleus incident team. Here are the basics:
  – the chief executive or CEO
  – the communications guru
  – the spokesperson
  – two board directors
  – a non-executive
  – the person responsible for security
  – two people with keyboard and secretarial skills
  – the maintenance or 'handyman'
  – someone who knows about the switchboard.
- Tell them what you expect of them.
- Run an annual practice or exercise so they get used to the idea.
- Make sure you know where to contact the team on a 24-hour basis – keep the database up to date. Make it someone's specific responsibility.
- Develop good relations with other organisations likely to be involved. That includes local authorities, train operators, police, fire, schools, etc.
- Get to know your communications opposite numbers, compare notes and share ideas.
- Link in with those key partners' own emergency strategies to ensure you know how your organisation is meant to fit in with their planning and vice versa.
- Keep the communications press database up to date – allocate it as a specific responsibility to an individual.

When the incident happens

- Call the team together.
- Find out exactly what happened – make it someone's specific task. They should be senior and know the organisation well.
- Consider co-opting anyone with specialist knowledge whose expertise might be valuable.
- Confirm and announce who the spokesperson is. They may not have anything to say immediately, but let everyone know who they will be dealing with.

- Stop, step back and evaluate the information – how much do you know?
- Prepare a holding statement. Stick to the facts; day, date, time, confirmation of the incident. If it involves casualties, how many, generally what's wrong with them/injuries, etc.
- Sketch out the action plan:
  - immediate remedial action
  - contact with the press
  - contact with relatives
  - possible security implications on site and at the homes of people involved
  - prevention measures
  - next steps.
- Get the team's agreement.
- Is an enquiry needed?
- Who will head it up?

Agree

- Press statement, who will deliver it and where?

Consider the impact on staff

- If the incident is outside working hours – do you need to contact staff, before they hear about it on the radio?
- Do key people need to be brought in?
- Consider briefing the staff.
- Make sure the switchboard operators are up to speed with as much as you can tell them.
- Have them keep a log of all calls – for future reference.
- Consider refreshments, meals and breaks.

Press

- Get the press off the 'doorstep'.
- Find them a pleasant room with refreshments, access to the toilets.
- Don't worry too much in the first instance about press phone lines as most use mobiles, but access to mains power is a boon.

- Ensure all contact is through the spokesperson. Avoid the temptation for the boss to step in.
- Avoid press pressure by announcing a press briefing time. Be sure to stick to the time and be punctual.
- Consider programme deadlines.
- If you hold a press conference:
  - pick a bright room that is big enough
  - put a screen behind the spokesperson if possible with the organisation's logo on it
  - try and arrange a PA system
  - put a big table in front of the spokesperson with room for everyone's microphones and recorders.

Revisit

- Security issues.
- Public enquiry line – contact BT they have an emergency line service – the contact point should be in your database!

Wait there is more!

- Prepare an action card – aide-mémoire.
- Have a press office tool kit box always at the ready containing all those stationery items you'll need in a hurry but won't have time to look for, as well as ready-made direction signs (press room, media briefing suite, etc.), press tabards or badges, contact lists, walkie-talkies.
- Have an area ready allocated for the media to park and make it large enough to accommodate an outside broadcast unit van.
- Make sure your own command centre is near to the press room and that it has been equipped.
- Know your local public.
- Keep your switchboard informed and part of the plan.
- Provide media training skills for those who will front the organisation – use those training sessions to identify who are the solid performers and who are weak.

The media works 24 hours a day

- Arrange for 24-hour cover to deal with them.
- Have back-up for if the lead spokesperson or communications lead is unavailable.
- Have a media minder
  - tea, coffee, generally supplied with comforts, technical support, link between them and lead communications person.

More preparation . . .

- Site the press room sensibly – avoid having it en route through the main entrance or A&E department and ensure that you can control the access points to it.
- Ensure the media room can be equipped technically with telephones (although in the first instance they can make do with mobiles, even though this breaks every hospital rule in the book), faxes, photocopier, e-mail access.
- Set aside a room suitable for press conferences.
- Don't forget, appropriate backdrops and logos.

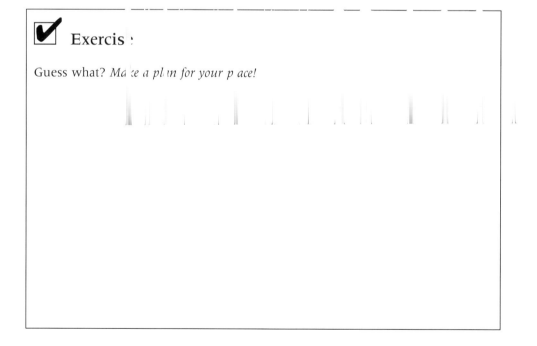

✔ **Exercise**

Guess what? *Make a plan for your place!*

Little things matter

- Prepare signs directing journalists and camp followers to media room and press conference suite.
- Think about the media's comfort
  – tea, coffee and sandwiches, parking, toilets!

WHEN MOST OF IT HITS THE FAN!

Practise this so it is no surprise.

- Get the team together.
- Establish the facts.
- Decide what you can say.
- BE HONEST.
- Brief support staff – especially switchboard and security staff.
- If the incident is criminal, inform police and coordinate lines.
- Contact communications leads in emergency services, local authority, health authority and regional office, head office, government departments.
- Brief key contacts quickly (don't forget your local MP).
- Develop a holding statement.
- Think about tone: compassionate, concerned, reassuring, sympathetic.
- Avoid blaming.
- Action: say what you are doing, reviewing procedures, taking in casualties, setting up an incident line, appealing for blood.

Yup, understand!

When EVERYTHING hits the fan!

- Information voids will be filled! So find out what's happening, fast and reliably – get someone on the case!
- Provide regular factual updates.
- Press conferences if appropriate.
- If casualties are involved, remember,

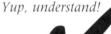 **Hazard Warning**
Information voids will be filled! So find out what's happening, fast and reliably – get someone on the case!

they probably won't like to hear gory details from medics – separate the press conferences for those being treated and for those providing the care.

- Demand a pool system for TV footage to avoid unnecessary disruption.
- Agree ground rules and be tough!

OK, THAT'S THE GAMEKEEPERS TAKEN CARE OF, WHAT ABOUT THE POACHERS?

Now's the time for you to understand what the press will be doing while you are playing with your plan. They'll have plans of their own!

The press will go through three stages.

The first thing the press will want is the answer to the Five 'W's. Funnily enough – so will you!

Stage one

The five Ws are: What, Who, Where, When and Why. They will be busting a gut to meet their deadlines with a first pass at the story. What happened, who was involved, where did it happen, when and a stab at the million dollar question – why?

Next they've got to turn events into something we can all understand – that means calling on the services of an expert!

Stage two

They will start by having the incident, or whatever it is, covered by whoever is nearest. Just rush to the scene and suss out what's going on. They will then move the story to their in-house journo expert (transport, environment, health, home affairs, media, court correspondent or whatnot). Next, they look for an expert to give an opinion. Usually an academic or perhaps the representative of a trade body, consumer group, user group, patient group, trades union – there's always someone around who will chip in their two pennyworth.

Now they have to make the story – this is the bit that pleases the journalist's profession and usually annoys the hell out of everyone involved. It jumps the gun and tries to do the job of an enquiry or a court. Speculation is rife and this is when the journalist is under pressure and at his or her most dangerous. They will be talking to neighbours, infiltrating buildings, digging up the past and burying reputations.

Stage three

Apportion blame! Find someone to hang the problem on. Whose fault was it?

CAN YOU WORK TOGETHER?

Why not? Unless you've done something really daft, or there are sensible reasons why the whole of the events cannot be made transparent, you can work with the media. How?

Easy. Recognise the media have needs too:

- The media have deadlines to meet – *remember them.*
- They have a job to do – *facilitate them.*
- They want clear factual briefings – *be honest.*
- If you are to be their key contact – **be accessible.**

They need pictures – help them find the ones they want, or they will simply publish the ones they can get. If they want a picture of the boss, better to have it of the person sitting down looking composed and like they know what they're doing, rather than legging it across the car park, pretending to be invisible, with a copy of the *Daily Blab* on their head. They don't have to speak, or say anything, just look human.

Maybe you have library of pictures of your key people – a good communications person would have thought about it; have them in black and white, colour and saved in JPEG or digital format for transmission over the Internet.

You may have a video of the organisation at work, or a copy of a your annual report. Techno-wizards can cut and paste all that kind of stuff and use it for their needs.

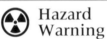 **Hazard Warning**
Remember to get the consent of the person being photographed. This is very important in the public sector, particularly for the NHS. Patients are protected by rules about privacy. You can't photograph them in their night shirt or lying on a bed, without their expressed consent. If they are elderly and frail, or unable to give *informed* consent, you can try and get it from a relative. However, it is a minefield of problems. Beware!

No sense in hiding it if it is in the public domain – they'll just use it and sort copyright details out later. They have deadlines to meet – remember?

NOT QUITE A CRISIS BUT A $£**&% NUISANCE

PREPARING FOR A VISIT FROM A VIP

If your crisis has involved loss of life – a Paddington or Lewisham – expect to have to deal with a VIP visit on top of all the other pressures you are dealing with.

> Perhaps it's not a crisis but the commissioning or opening of something new. No matter, it's all the same set of rules.

However, let's look on the bright side. A visit can cheer everyone up, reward performance and be a pat on the back for the people who have done their best. They are also a great photo opportunity.

VIPs love to get in on the act

Politicians are a bit different. If your local MP expects their visit to be treated like a royal visit, you've got the wrong MP. They are supposed to visit and find out what the real world is like. Don't put out the red carpet. A ministerial visit is a bit different. They can't leave the office without a secretary, a political advisor, a person from the press department, a regional top-brass, a driver and a policeman. Can't really treat that like it was your auntie popping in!

Royal visits send folk apoplectic

Here are some key points for a VIP visit:

- VIPs are photo opportunities – get the local, regional and national press turned out, with photographers.
- VI VIPs will have press officers. Liaise with them, let them do the work! Be sure to learn from the experience.
- Be on the safe side, have your own photographer

Gotcha!

present, taking the pictures *you* want – give them clear instructions.

- Make sure you have good contact with local police and special branch – royals have their own detective in tow and the Royal Protection Squad are the ones in £3000 suits with deaf-aids in their ears.
- If the visit is from a politician, think about the potential for a demonstration from some group or other. Be sure to advise the police.
- Restrict the welcoming party – everyone will think of a reason for being in the hand-shaking party. It may be your job to think of a rationale about who can't be there. Clear it with the boss!
- If the visit involves patients or users of a service, restrict the others around to front-line staff only and be sure to get picture consent.
- If it looks like turning into a scrum, make the press agree to a pool arrangement where one TV crew and one photographer is allowed on to the ward or restricted area, to avoid disruption.

HERE ARE THE GOLDEN DOS AND DON'TS IN DEALING WITH YOUR NEW FRIENDS IN THE PRESS

DON'T

Got it!

- Go off the record – consider everything you tell the press is on the record. That way there's no confusion and you won't get into a mess. As you gain experience you can start thinking about off the record briefings unattributable comments, but it is a minefield. Beware!
- Tell 'porkies' – not even smart, technical, weasly worded ones. They all come back to haunt you. If you can't answer the question because you don't have the information, say so. Agree a course of action and a time to get back with the answer – and be sure you stick to it. If you can't answer the question for a good

reason, such as issues of confidentiality, or legal reasons, say so. The press are trained in the legal stuff and will know how far they can push you. If there are other reasons, say something like: *'There are factors surrounding that question that makes it impossible for me to answer it.'* The next question will be; what factors are they, then? Your only answer is: *'I am not able to go into them.'* If you are pressed just keep repeating the same answer.

- Exaggerate – the press just like the facts. It is the subeditor's job to do the exaggeration!
- Speculate – don't pretend you know if you don't and don't try and be a forecaster, unless that is your job.
- Comment about others involved – here's the standard phrase: *'You'll have to ask them about that . . .'*.
- Say 'no comment' – the worst phrase in the communications dictionary.
- Wait to be asked for information – if you've got additional information, make it available as soon as you can.
- Lose your temper – go home and kick the dustbin instead.
- Let non-team members speak to the press – pick a spokesperson and stay with them.

Do

Done it!

- Give background briefings – this is a great way to build media relations and trust. Communicate in the good times and have something in the bank for the bad times.
- Be open and honest – if the press think you are straight with them, nine times out of ten, they will be straight with you. They have a job to do but they recognise it is easier to do the job with someone they can trust and that trust is a two way thing.
- Be accessible and available – this means handing over phone numbers, extension numbers, home phone numbers, mobile phone numbers, pager numbers and e-mail addresses. That's called communication – sorry!

- Be first to give information – if you have it and you can, hand it over. This is a great relationship-builder and saves everyone a lot of time.
- Meet deadlines – find out what they are. Ask 'When do you need this by?' And, deliver.
- Avoid conflict – no one wins a punch-up with the press.
- Be friendly and helpful – just like that nice person in your favourite store.
- Facilitate, help the media do their job – if you are the communications guru, it is *your* job.
- Post-match enquiry – measure everything that is measurable.
- Evaluate how you performed – be honest, did you play a blinder, or fumble the ball?
- Assess whether the coverage reflected your key messages – are you getting over the image you want? How do you know?
- Ask the media how they felt they were treated – go on, we dare you!
- Ask staff – why not, its their place of work, too.
- Ask your key contacts – the ones in your database – 'How was it for you?'
- Revise your crisis strategy – then revise it again.

 Exercise

- Revise your communications strategy. What do you mean you've not written it yet?

INTERNAL STUFF

*Networking is what you do in the firm's time, gossip is what you
do in your own time. Or, is it the other way around?*

COMMUNICATING ON THE INSIDE

All organisations, big and small have communication needs. For some, word
of mouth is enough. For others, not even the word of God can be heard
above the din of the day to day.

Communicating management messages, dealing with gossip, being sure
the right things are heard and the wrong ones are switched off is a task for
the communications guru. Just like communicating externally, the internal
job requires planning, preparing and an in-built mechanism that allows you
to listen, learn and act.

The target audience is different but the techniques are the same. High-
quality internal communications strategies are the hallmark of successful
organisations. It shows that people in the organisation matter. It encourages
teamwork and is the biggest aid to organisation efficiency outside the
invention of the shredder!

SOME IDEAS ABOUT MANAGING THE
INTERNAL MESSAGE

COMMUNICATION DAYS

Got something really important to tell the staff? Do it face to face. Big job?
Yup! But if the message is important enough it's worth doing properly.
Here's how you organise a communications day.

This needs the boss and the most senior person involved with the project or issue you want the staff to know about. Break the staff into manageable groups and brief them personally. Start the briefings first thing in the morning and repeat them on the hour, every hour throughout the day, until everyone has heard the story first-hand. This is a tiring and time-consuming way to communicate, but it is magic. Everyone gets the same message, from the horse's mouth. No gossip, no speculation. 'Just the facts – ma'am'.

FAMILY OPEN DAYS

Great for organisational image and breaking down barriers. Be sure to get the local press along. Open days are very good PR. Be sure to send the kids home happy, with a balloon and a tummy full of jelly!

NEWSLETTERS

If you work with a Camilla or a Nigel, who says; '*I've got a great idea. Let's have a staff newsletter and call it the Grape Vine*', you have our permission to stab them, put their bodies in a sack full of bricks and throw them in the river. It is not a crime to murder the Grape Vine people of this world. Honest!

Communicators of the world, please wake up to the fact that staff newsletters of the Grape Vine variety do not get read. They get binned, or used to line the bottom of a budgie's cage. Good newsletters work, but they've got to be good. And, that means time, skill, effort and the money to do it well.

Think about it. If your place is a big organisation employing lots of people doing lots of different jobs, we bet they all read different newspapers. They'll read anything from the *Financial Times* to the *Daily Star*. So how can you expect to get the attention of everyone, with one style of newsletter?

If your place is a small place, what do you need a newsletter for? Try talking to people!

Ask yourself these questions

- Who is the newsletter for and how does that impact on the design – usually newspaper styles rather than magazine styles do better in readership retention tests.
- Who will write, edit and produce it? It is a proper job, putting a good newsletter together!

- Who decides what goes in it? The editor, a committee, the boss? Is it a management bugle or the real voice of and for the team?
- How often can you fill it up with things that people will want to read. If it's once a quarter it is a history book. If it's once a week it's a newspaper and it will cost a fortune.
- Who will pay for it? Will it contain advertising? Who will sell the advertising?

 We're waiting! Got the answers?

Still want to 'do a newsletter'? Remember this:

- Keep it simple. Desktop publishing is fun, but in the wrong hands, useless. Don't use 20 **typefaces,** *just* **because** you've *got* them.
- Make it punchy. More people read the *Sun* than *The Times.*
- Create a sense of ownership – let everyone have their say.
- Print complaints and compliments – side by side.
- Don't let the boss hog the space.
- Get as close to a newspaper format as possible.
- Pictures bring the printed word to life.
- Timing and frequency are crucial.

HERE ARE THE BASICS FOR PUTTING TOGETHER A NEWSLETTER

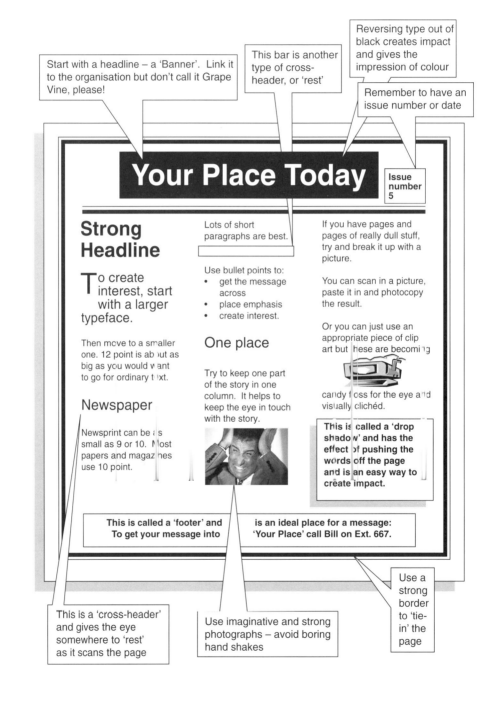

Start with a headline – a 'Banner'. Link it to the organisation but don't call it Grape Vine, please!

This bar is another type of cross-header, or 'rest'

Reversing type out of black creates impact and gives the impression of colour

Remember to have an issue number or date

Your Place Today

Issue number 5

Strong Headline

To create interest, start with a larger typeface.

Then move to a smaller one. 12 point is about as big as you would want to go for ordinary text.

Newspaper

Newsprint can be as small as 9 or 10. Most papers and magazines use 10 point.

Lots of short paragraphs are best.

Use bullet points to:
- get the message across
- place emphasis
- create interest

One place

Try to keep one part of the story in one column. It helps to keep the eye in touch with the story.

If you have pages and pages of really dull stuff, try and break it up with a picture.

You can scan in a picture, paste it in and photocopy the result.

Or you can just use an appropriate piece of clip art but these are becoming

candy floss for the eye and visually clichéd.

This is called a 'drop shadow' and has the effect of pushing the words off the page and is an easy way to create impact.

This is called a 'footer' and To get your message into

is an ideal place for a message: 'Your Place' call Bill on Ext. 667.

This is a 'cross-header' and gives the eye somewhere to 'rest' as it scans the page

Use imaginative and strong photographs – avoid boring hand shakes

Use a strong border to 'tie-in' the page

WHAT ABOUT NOTICE BOARDS?

Move a little closer to the page: here's a communications secret. No one takes any notice of notice boards. Why? For the same reason you don't notice the stain on the hall carpet or the piece of wallpaper peeling up at the edges in the bathroom. You don't see how grubby the car seats have got and you don't notice you need a haircut.

All of these things grow on you, creep up on you and blur into the invisible. We just don't see them any more. We work in invisible organisations.

Notice boards are invisible. Check 'em out. Most will have out-of-date notices, notices pinned on top of notices and many will have trades union and staff announcements in public areas – entirely inappropriate for public consumption.

HOW TO GET NOTICE BOARDS NOTICED

First the greatest trick of all – move them! Have notice boards on easels, or legs and shift them around. Move them to the other side of the corridor. Put them at the bottom of the stairs. Shift them all the time. People will say: *what's that doing over there*? And, the chances are they will read what's on it.

What else:

- Be ruthless about what goes on them and even more ruthless about what comes off them. Make a 'ten-day rule'. Nothing should be on a notice board for more than ten days. Any longer and you need a different way to manage that message.
- Have all messages dated with the day they were first displayed. Count to ten and bin them!
- Provide a generous supply of tacks or pins.
- Don't mix messages – public notices on public boards and staff messages on staff boards.
- Make someone responsible for maintaining the board.
- Just because it's a notice doesn't mean it can't be well designed – impose some creative criteria on what can get displayed.
- Print the rule for the use of the board in the top right hand corner – that can stay for longer than ten days!

GOSSIP

This is a killer. Gossip screws up ideas, causes unnecessary anxiety and eats
away at the inside of the organisation. It is corrosive. Good research into
gossip as part of organisational dynamics is not easy to come by. Some of the
best was done, in the mid-1990s by Jorgan Vedin, the future-ologist and
management guru, who was working with what was then Astra
Pharmaceuticals, now Astra-Zeneca.

He demonstrated that everyday, in a large organisation, one person would
have meaningful dialogue with 15 colleagues and that each of those 15
would have dialogue with another 15 and so on. Now you begin to
understand the dynamics of gossip – it is as powerful as a forest fire. This
is what the compounding effect of the 15 × 15 looks like, starting on
Monday through Friday.

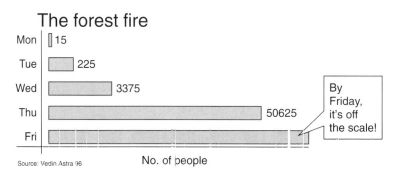

WHAT TO DO ABOUT IT?

* Start some gossip of your own – get out from behind your desk, talk to
  people, tell 'em the facts, offer them your opinion. Good or bad, get the
  news into the organisation on your terms.
* Be open and encourage openness amongst colleagues. Have a real
  open-door policy. If your door is open anyone can come in and ask a
  question. If the door is shut they'll respect your privacy. But maybe
  they'll be forced to speculate about the facts with colleagues!
* Listen to the opinion formers and gossips – talk to them before they talk
  to the others.
* Get news into the public domain as fast as you can. If there is gossip
  about something you can't yet speak about, tell the staff you are aware

of their concerns and will make a statement, or talk to them at an agreed time – and stick to it.

CHANGE!

Everyone likes progress – it's change they don't like!

If ever there was a reason to have a communications guru on board it is at times of change. Uncertainty, worry, concerns about redundancy, paying the mortgage and meeting the bills, it's all at the heart of communications.

HERE ARE THE TEN COMMANDMENTS OF COMMUNICATIONS AT A TIME OF CHANGE:

1   **If it's worth telling, tell it fast.** There is no excuse and no reason not to get organised and make sure everyone who needs to know, knows. Who needs to know? It is a safe assumption that everyone needs to know! Communication days, walk-about's, get out from behind your desk – you can do it. You gotta do it. No excuses.

2   **Communicate everyday, face to face, not videos, notice boards, newsletters.** There are a whole load of communication devices available to organisations but best of all is face to face. There is a great phrase, it's one of those sayings that you would expect a student of Confucius to recite. It says: *People who work out of doors know which way the wind is blowing.* The message is simple, get out from behind the desk, get out of doors, talk to people on the ground and find out which way the wind is blowing!

3   **Distinguish communication from information.** Circulating a pile of numbers, statistics and graphs is a neat trick and thoroughly understood by the folk that send them out. Unfortunately, they are seldom understood, or appreciated, by the people who read them. If the message includes information, statistics or budgets, be sure to include a written commentary explaining them and what they mean for the organisation, the department and the luckless individual reading the stuff, trying to find out!

4   **Listen as well as talk.** It's an old chestnut and a terrible cliché but we can't resist it. *You have one mouth and two ears, use them in that proportion.* Sorry, but how better to underline the fact that communications is not just about delivering messages, it is about capturing messages. How do you know what the organisation wants to know if you don't ask and listen to the answers?

5   **Communicate in the good times and build credibility for the bad times.** So often communications gurus will get called in to sort out a mess that could so easily have been avoided. If organisations would invest in a regular stream of information cascading through the departments they could build up trust. When the bad times come – and they come to every organisation in the end – there is a pool of trust that makes it much easier to deliver difficult messages and helps them to fall into receptive ears. Invest in communications and it will pay you back, handsomely.

6   **Train everyone to be a communicator.** If you depend on cascading information into the organisation through a management structure it is vital that the managers, who are the links in the chain, are on board and trained as communicators. Picture the scene. A manager is back from a briefing from his boss and is about to address his colleagues. '*Well*' he says, '*this is what they want us to do now*'. To destroy the message, all he has to do is raise an eyebrow at the end of the statement! Look in the mirror, do it and see how powerful that one gesture can be. All your hard work is down the tubes. More than that is the damage that talk outside the organisation can do. Public sector employees, under pressure from system users, meet at parties and social gatherings. It is easy to admit their service is a basket case! At times of trouble give your staff the answers and turn them into ambassadors.

7   **Communicate more rather than less.** There is a seventies joke that goes: How often should I kiss my wife? Answer: before someone else does! How often should you communicate? Answer: before someone else does. Communication should not be regular and routine. It should be discontinuous, as and when needed. It should be surprising and exciting. It should be varied in tone and texture, volume and shade. And above all, constant.

8   **Always tell the truth.** This is not easy. The truth is sometimes difficult to know and sometimes damaging and inappropriate to tell. The real issue here is don't tell a lie. If you can't say, then say why you can't. Either you don't know or you can't tell. If you can't tell, explain you

cannot tell and promise a time that you can – and stick to it. We can wait for the truth, but few of us have any time for liars.

9   **Not from on high but the heart**. A message to the boss. You are as intent on doing your job as anyone else. You do the best you can do and so does everyone else. If you have something to say, tell it truthfully and from the heart, and most important of all . . .

10 **Let people read it in your eyes**. Not in a memo, not in an e-mail but, whenever you can, face to face!

THE POWER OF THE HAND-WRITTEN NOTE

The next bit is about e-mail so this is a good time to remind you of the power of a hand-written note!

As we come to depend more and more on internal e-mail systems, make a rule . . . make a rule to send at least one hand-written note a day. Send one of those sticky jotter thingamajigs.

A note that says thanks, or well done, has such a powerful impact. Circulate a note that says: 'Sally wrote this report, isn't it good'. Remember birthdays, anniversaries, the dates that people joined the organisation and send a note. It has the impact of a tonne of TNT. People have come not to expect a hand-written note.

Reinvent it. Keep some blank cards in your drawer and send one to someone once a week. If you can't find a reason – invent one. If you can't invent one, you're working in the wrong place!

WHAT ABOUT E-MAIL?

If you agree that most organisations are very good at getting themselves into a mess over IT, computers and technology, believe us, you 'ain't seen nothin' yet! There is another disaster waiting just around the corner. The millennium bug was a flea bite by comparison. The message is: it is the messages that will cause the problem.

In the NHS, patient appointments, pathology results, internal messaging, ordering and countless other tasks are set to become electronic. All GPs will be hooked up with e-mail, as will most managers and hospital consultants.

 **Hazard Warning**

If experiences in the private sector are anything to go by, the NHS has no idea what it is letting itself in for with e-mail.

Litigation, writs and battles are just an e-mail away. The problems will start internally and then the outside world will come crashing down on the heads of unsuspecting NHS management.

What's it like over at your place? Are you any different?

The potential for problems identified itself in the USA in March 1999. It was reported that the merchant bankers Morgan Stanley, Dean Witter & Co. agreed an out-of-court settlement with two of its employees.

Reason? Some other staff had circulated a bad-taste joke about African-Americans on the internal e-mail system. The aggrieved staff reached for their lawyers and the company reached for its cheque book.

The court was about to decide that employers are responsible for all internal e-mail traffic, regardless of its origination. Morgan's, apparently, settled. This is just part of what the NHS can expect and maybe your organisation, too.

Other lawsuits alleging everything from sexual discrimination to breach of confidence have been sparked by companies without proper e-mail policies and planning.

Industry has been caught unprepared by the impact of e-mail. A Gallup poll conducted in the USA found that the typical office worker in a decent-sized corporation would deal with up to 60 incoming and outgoing e-mails in a day. There are about 156 000 administrative and estates staff in the NHS (to say nothing of the doctors and nurses). That could mean, when they all get the hang of e-mail, there is a potential for nine million messages to whizz around the system, every day. Controlling the content of all of the messages is an impossible job.

What is the message potential where you work?

Should an employer become involved in a court case or an industrial tribunal, electronic mail is ready to provide some more shocks. A legal device known as 'discovery' can be used to force litigants to reveal every file, note and piece of paper they have that might be pertinent to the case in question. Nothing may be hidden. Courts can prize open your filling cabinets and archives.

 **Hazard Warning**

Planting a blank e-mail into a file history makes it possible, at a later stage, to go back and fill it in with any message you like. A trick likely to fool everyone, even an experienced observer.

They can plug into your hard disk, too. If the records they want to see include e-mail messages that have been deliberately erased or modified, you might find yourself in contempt of court.

Industry is spending millions setting up record management systems, policies and organisational structures to manage the invisible tide of e-mail.

The simple answer? Treat electronic messages like paper messages and file them – the gurus call it *E-archiving*. Unfortunately, this is not so simple. Deciding what to keep and what to dump becomes a major problem. What to retain and how long for, is a policy decision the boss may have to answer for, in court or at the Public Accounts Committee. (*Time to buy a smart new suit!*).

E-mails can easily be faked or fiddled with and printed-out messages can be similarly counterfeited. A storage system that is tamper-proof does not come cheap and will eat up a storage disk faster that an American termite can chomp its way through a house.

So-called e-shredding software exists and is one way of zapping messages that could come back to haunt you. However, hidden 'history' and cache files in Windows and other systems can leave a trail of clues that the determined computer literate can follow. Emptying the 'recycle bin' does not mean 'gone for good'. E-mail will become fundamental to the way we run our affairs. Here are some outline rules and guidance.

Six ideas to avoid e-fail with e-mail

1 Warn all staff, with an 'on-screen' message about the organisation's rules for e-mail.

Check!

2 Make it clear that e-mail is not confidential and will be routinely monitored. More importantly, hammer home the fact that e-mail is not a substitute for the kind of conversation that used to take place in the canteen, lavatory or lift.

3 Stamp out digital gossip; bar the transmission of personal mail, jokes, smutty material and non-business messages. American experience shows staff who are offended can sue their employer – someone is bound to try a case here, sooner or later.

4 Set up in-house e-training to help staff understand the rules. This might persuade a court that you have taken your responsibilities seriously. Incorporate e-mail policies into contracts of employment.

5 Install one of the new programmes to monitor e-mail for key words and phrases, to flag up offensive material.

6   Decide on archive policies now: what to keep, how long
    to keep it, how to keep it and who is responsible. Cost
    electronic archive processes and budget for it – the
    outlay is more than you think. Disk and tape space
    doesn' come cheap. But not as expensive as a few days
    at the High Court!

☢ Hazard Warning

Never, never, never, never, never, never, never, never, never, never,
never, never, never, open an attachment to an e-mail that has the suffix
.EXE – unless it came from your mother and even then be suspicious.
These types of file are a favourite vehicle for the lunatics who spread
viruses.

Come to think of it, don't open any attachment to an e-message if you
have no idea who the sender is. These days the lunatics can infect your
machine with word-processing files and all manner of other stuff. Virus
checker software is available and can be easily updated via the Internet.
Your communications strategy should ensure that incoming traffic is
filtered through a central point that automatically scans for virus infection
of attachments.

PUBLIC SPEAKING, MAKING A PRESENTATION AND HOW TO WOW THE AUDIENCE!

You can be really good at this! We insist!

Public speaking is easy. People have turned up and want to hear what you
have to say. The organisers want to have a success on their hands and they
want you to do well. You want to do your bit and your Mum thinks you're
lovely!

You've got everything going for you! Let's get into this . . .

THE TEN COMMANDMENTS OF PRIZE-WINNING PRESENTATIONS

1   See yourself as others see you, don't look at what you see in the mirror.
    Find people you trust to critique what you do. Record yourself, tape

yourself and listen to yourself. What do you like? What don't you like? Be honest with yourself and you will get better.

2   Be clear about your message. What are your objectives? What message do you want to get across and what image do you want to portray? What are you going to achieve?

3   Start by painting an overall picture of what your message is. Get people into the same groove as you!

4   Plan the route of your presentation. Map out the journey. Build up to your main points. Take the audience with you.

5   You know your stuff and you know your message. Help your audience. Headline what you are doing and include signposts about your direction.

6   Practise/rehearse, but bear in mind you are giving your thoughts, judgements and opinions – not putting on a show.

7   Win the hearts, then win the minds. Attitude is the best persuader. Try and win the person and not the argument.

8   Keep it simple. Even if you have a complicated message, boil it down. Remember the communications triangle – three points to explain the most complicated thing!

9   Be an enthusiast. If you don't like what you do, how will anyone else?

10 Be you! You are unique, a one-off. Folk have come a long way to listen to you. Be nervous sure, but use the energy to be SUPER YOU!

HERE'S THE SECRET OF GOOD PUBLIC SPEAKING

Think Audience

Yup, it's as easy as that!

They want to hear you and they want to know what you know – so sock it to them. Give 'em what they want!

• Be sure of you objective. Do you want to: convert/inform/persuade/inspire/entertain/provoke/whaderyerwannado?

• Know your subject and your content. The content wins the minds and the presentation wins the hearts. But, none of it works if you don't know the subject. Don't be flattered into talking about stuff you don't know about.

• Find out about the audience. If you're not absolutely sure about who you are talking to, do the obvious thing. Ask! Say: 'My name is Freda Smart-Person and I am the boss of This Place-is-Us, I understand some of you

are engineers, some of you are accountants, some of you are brain surgeons . . .
Just so I can get my thinking straight, can I ask the engineers to put up their
hands, and now the . . .'. Get the picture?

- Figure out why they are there. What do they want to hear from you –
  and sock it to them. You'll have done well if they remember 10% of
  what you say!
- Keep it to the KISS principle. Keep It Simple, Stupid. Old yet good
  advice. Make your points, point in the direction of the conclusion.
- Check your flow. Allow the audience to catch up with your brain
  waves! Use headlines, summaries and signposts.

Tell 'em what you're gonna tell 'em. Tell 'em. Tell 'em again and repeat it!
  Here's a start: *'I'm going to look at how we can influence our daily lives. There*
are three main issues: effort, help and hope. So first, let me start with effort . . .'. See,
easy!

BE A PROFESSIONAL

- Stick to time. Take your watch off and place it in your eye-line, where
  you can be sure to see it. Pace yourself and always finish on time. Only
  amateurs over-run. Practise timings.
- Rehearse! Rehearse out loud and time yourself. Stand up. Do t on your
  feet – at least once. Be familiar with your material. Tape it an listen to
  yourself – that's what the professionals do.

PREPARATION

- Plan the story – the beginning, the middle and the end. Be clear about
  what you want to say.
- Prepare your presentation in the spoken word – not the written word.
  Forget the grammar (*Like this book – Ed*), concentrate on getting the
  message across.
- Work to the three 'I' rule: Interest, Inform, Involve.
- Do your homework, research your subject, and make it interesting and
  relevant to the audience; use anecdotes, quotes and stories.
- Break the speech up. Have 'punctuation marks'. Try and get some
  response from the audience. Ask them questions, or to vote on a
  subject: *'How many of you think that's right?'*

- Use the introduction to open the line of communication between you and the audience. Position yourself in their minds. Say: *'The reason I am here today is following the article I had published in the Blogg's* Journal of Brain Surgery. *I want to develop that thinking and share with you my latest ideas'*.
- No matter how good you are, the audience is not up to remembering more than three main messages. So don't waste your time on anything else!
- Have a conclusion. Build to a climax and involve the audience in a decision. Send 'em home whistling a familiar tune.
- Cut out all of the jargon phrases – even to a professional audience.

NOTE OR NOT TO NOTES – THAT IS THE QUESTION?

Yup you'll need notes . . .

You will need verbatim notes if you are a jolly posh person and the press are hanging on your every word and the Prime Minister will give you the sack if you say something relaxed and off-message.

Apart from prepared speeches, you can have any note format you are comfortable with. Key words, phrases, pictures – anything.

Some speeches have to be delivered with great care and the press are given copies of what you (or your boss says), in advance. Be sure to mark across the top:

CHECK AGAINST DELIVERY

This is journo-pro-speak for: This is what we expect them to say but they may deviate! So, pay attention!

Otherwise:

- If you use notes, don't hold them in your hands, unless you absolutely have to. Your hands may shake and the paper will tremble and you will look like a nervous wreck!
- Beware of cards; they are fussy and slide down a lectern.
- Handwriting is, in times of stress, always unreadable. Use a word processor.

- Use a lectern and slide your notes across, from one side to the other, don't turn them over.
- Number the pages of your notes – in case you drop them, just before you are going to do your stuff. That way you stand half a chance of getting them back in the right order!
- Look at your notes openly, don't try and sneak a view, or peek at them. You'll look furtive!
- If you use notes on A4 paper, or are reading a speech from a full text, don't have it typed to the bottom of the page. Why? Because as you read to the bottom your head will drop down and the audience will get sick of the view of the top of your head! Top third only, bottom two thirds blank. And:

Use a nice, big, clear, typeface

NEXT, PREPARE YOURSELF AND THE ROOM

- A big presentation, something that is important? You will use up a trillion calories, so, if you can, rest before you are 'on'.
- Think about what you are going to wear – be appropriately dressed.
- Always have a lectern if you can. Pre-check the height. It is supposed to be something to put your notes o not a barrier between you and the audience.
- Always use a microphone. Even i he room is small, a microphone gives a 'presence' to your voice.
- If you are confident and want to alk abou (doing an Anne Widdecombe), then make sure y are wired up with a radio 'nic'.
- Record what you do – and use th tape to arn about yoursel and to get better.
- Check the lights. Can you see your notes? Are the lights in your eyes?
- Of course, you won't always have time for all the pre-checks – so make it your business to get as much information as you can in advance from the organisers of the event. If you don't, then you only have yourself to blame!

DAZZLING DELIVERY? HERE'S HOW . . .

- Enjoy being nervous. Enjoy yourself and channel all that energy into your performance.

- Talk to the audience, don't read a speech at them.
- Make regular eye contact with the audience.
- Watch the audience and respond to their mood.
- Moving about is distracting unless you have arranged for a following spotlight in a darkened auditorium (*a favourite Roy Lilley technique*).
- Make sure the audience can hear you.
- Finish on time.
- Judge your delivery. Make 120 written words run to one minute and you are on course.
- Pause regularly – for effect, thinking time and tone.
- Use body language – let it speak for you. But, try not to be like an Italian traffic cop!
- If you get embarrassed, so will the audience.

QUESTIONS? SURE, TAKE 'EM ON THE CHIN! BUT, DON'T HAVE A ROW!

- Stay cool – you know your stuff. You are in command.
- Elaborate and illustrate.
- Be nice – even if the questioner is a pig! Say: '*I'm sorry you see it that way. What I'm trying to do here is to . . .*', or: '*I guess we'll have to agree to disagree*' – and smile!
- Be clear and simple but avoid being patronising – they aren't as smart as you. That's why you're answering the questions and they are asking them!

Avoid

- Apologies – for anything. Especially: 'This is not really my field'. If it isn't you shouldn't be there!
- Whining: 'In the short time available'; 'I didn't expect to be asked'; 'I'm standing in for . . .'. **If you can't hack it like a pro', get off!**
- I'm tired – I've just arrived from the next town, flown in from Moscow, driven from Manchester – who cares. Get on with it!
- Dithering – 'I think that's all I have to say'. Get a grip, you're the expert!

PRESENTATIONS?

It's all very easy. Ask that nice Mr Gates and his PowerPoint to do it for you!
(Or Star Office on Linex – Ed)

If you can't 'do' PowerPoint crawl away and die! PowerPoint is fast
becoming the industry standard. There is a tutorial that comes as part of
the software that will take you through the whole process. Instant expert.
Easy!

Here are some rules

• Use 'overheads' for audiences up to 40. After that, you will need to
  think about using PowerPoint, from a computer.
• Disable the computer's screen saver. It's annoying and could be
  embarrassing, if it pops up in the middle of a presentation.
• Use dark backgrounds and light-coloured words for PowerPoint and
  light backgrounds and dark-coloured words for overheads.
• It's best to stick to yellow words on a blue background for PowerPoint
  and black words on a white background for overheads.
• Disable the PowerPoint sound effects – they're for the kids.
• Use a title slide with your name and e-address, as a starter and finish
  slide. No e-address? Try knitting seaweed for a hobby . . .
• Make sure your contact details are on every slide. Go into the slide
  master and make sure it is part of the footer.
• Never let your speech follow the graphics. Use graphics to follow what
  you say.
• Never say:
  – 'As you can see on the slide . . .'
  – 'This slide shows . . .'
  – 'This slide isn't too clear, but . . .'.

GOT LOADSA DATA TO PRESENT?

Graphs look great when you carefully compose them on a computer screen,
but they invariably look like a load of rubbish when projected on to a big
screen. Do your graphs look like this:

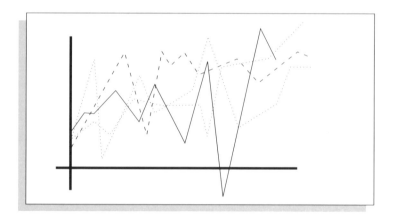

This is in black and white – think about the mess it would look in colour! Something like the map for the Prague tube network, or wiring diagram for a Soviet rocket launcher.

Solution? Some people use one of those annoying little hand-held laser pointer things, that projects a pinprick of light on to the screen. If you've got one of those things trash it! They are useless. There are two problems with them.

- If you use one you'll get into the habit of looking at the screen and not at the audience. Everyone will go home thinking you need a haircut, or your frock's too tight across the shoulders!
- The beam emphasises the slightest tremble in the hands and the little pinprick of light jumps around the screen and makes it look like you are very nervous (perhaps you are, but no point in advertising it) or you've got the early on-set of some desperate disease.

WHAT'S THE ANSWER?

If you can, use a bar chart instead of a line graph. That's one like this:

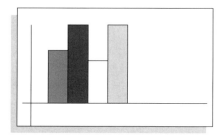

Better still . . .

LEARN TO DO A 'BUILD'

This is a neat facility that comes with PowerPoint. You construct the graph in the normal way but you display it on the screen, component by component, so the whole picture builds on the screen in front of the audience. This allows you the opportunity to say:

> 'First can I draw your attention to the red line – this represents the number of *whatever* . . .
>
> Now look at the green line *which is* . . .
>
> Now notice the blue line and *see the difference between* . . .'

The audience will sit spell bound as the lines snake across the screen! For the first time in their lives they will have understood a graph and been able to see the face of the speaker – presentation history in the making! You can do it with all types of charts, bar charts, pie charts and lines.

Here's how:

 Seven simple steps to chart heaven!   *Click!*

1   Draw your graph or chart in the normal way and finish and save.
2   Right-mouse click on the graph to highlight it.
3   Go to the tool bar and select 'Slide Show'.
4   When the box drops down, select 'Custom Animation'.
5   Select 'Chart Effects' – you can then choose to have your chart build by series, categories or elements. Play around with this and see from the preview button which effect suits you best.
6   Now select 'Timing'. You will see that you can have the changes occur at the command of a mouse click or automatically, and you can set the time between changes.
7   Press OK and you're finished.

Easy, eh? Charts to be proud of! Say 'thank you' to that nice Mr Gates.

 To disable the screen saver in Windows, go: *Right click on the desk top, select Properties, click the Screen Saver Tab, and select 'none'. Click apply and OK!*

THE ANNUAL REPORT

Reputation is a large bubble that bursts the moment you try and blow yourself up!

YOU'VE GOT TO DO ONE SO MAKE IT WORTHWHILE

The annual report is a chance to shine, show off and cover up the bits you're not too proud of. If you're lucky you may get away with it all!

Increasingly, the annual report is seen as a product of the communications department, team, or you. If producing the annual report is in your in-tray you're first job is to look at the latest guidance about what has to be included in it.

There was a time when financial information and a few pictures of bonny, bouncing, happy people was enough. Not true any more. Increasingly, government is holding the NHS to account and that accountability is expressed in the annual report.

So, question:

What are the statutory requirements that have to be included in the annual report?

Answer:

We dunno!

Well, that's not quite true. We do have a pretty good idea what's to go into them this year. There's stuff that's recommended to be there, stuff that should be there and stuff that's gotta be there. But, the problem is, it keeps changing. New stuff has to be included all the time. So, the answer is: let's find out. There are issues of financial and clinical governance to be included as well as workforce issues and goodness knows what else. There are four possible solutions:

1   Ask the finance director, the human resources director and the lead on clinical governance exactly what their latest requirement is, then check with the chief executive's office. (*Good, but time-consuming and they may not know.*)

> You can find the Department of Health Website (incidentally, it is very good indeed) at http://www.doh.gov.uk/dhhome.htm Then go to **publications**; then **coin** (Central Office of Information), **view circulars by series**, and then press the **search** button and enter what you are looking for.

2   Enquire at Region to see if they've done a distillation of the latest guidance. (*They usually know this sort of thing – it keeps 'em in business – but not always.*)

3   Go to the Department of Health web site, use the search engine and pull off all the guidance that relates to annual reports – then you'll be bang up to date. (*Very smart and you'll be the only one in the world who will really, really, really know.*)

4   Copy last year's report and hope no one notices. (*High-risk strategy and can be career limiting.*)

> If you've purchased this book just to find out how to do an annual report and feel cheated because there isn't a nice neat answer to the question about content, send the book back and ask for a refund. You won't get it but you can ask and it might make you feel better!

Seriously, we thought very hard about how to answer that question but as we hope the book will sell millions of copies and become the master-work on how to do communications, we just couldn't run the risk of putting something in that wasn't 100% correct or is likely to go past its sell-by date faster than a fresh prawn. Are we forgiven? Please, say yes!

Thank you!

NOW, HERE'S SOME STUFF WE ARE SURE ABOUT!

There's good news and bad.

The annual report does not have to contain the full accounts – all the boring number bits that only the anoraks can understand. A summary set in a specific formula will do.

Wow, that makes life a bit easier doesn't it? Yes it does, but here's the bad news.

You do still have to publish the full annual accounts and they have to be in a specific format. That format is described centrally but there is a good deal of flexibly in how the rules are interpreted. If there is any doubt about the format or content; ask your district auditor.

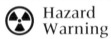 **Hazard Warning**
The auditor has the final say and you must seek their advice. Not all auditors see it the same way – so ask *your* auditor, not any auditor.

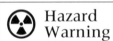 **Hazard Warning**
A summary of the accounts is not a substitute for publishing the full accounts, and when publishing a summary it is wise to include a phrase along the lines of:

'These accounts are a summary only and a copy of the full statutory accounts may be obtained, free, from . . . (telephone and name)'

Once you've figured out what goes in them, a job best done in conjunction with the finance tribe, they don't have to be an elaborate job. Photocopies will do, tidily bound or stapled; cheap and easy.

However, if you intend to include a summary of the accounts in the annual report, you'll want to think about the content of the summary (another question for the district auditor) and how to present it to the majority of readers, who will find a balance sheet about as good as Mogadon for staying awake.

To compare your performance with last year, or several previous years, think about the use of graphs. A pie chart is always easy to understand and makes an impact.

 Think Box
This is not about patronising people, or making fun of folk who are not at ease with rows and columns of numbers. This is about you getting the message across. If they don't understand it, you've not done it!

OK, SO NOW THE GRUNGE IS OUT OF THE WAY, WHAT ABOUT THE OTHER BITS?

Why do an annual report? It's partly about governance and partly about bragging. Governance, because it is public money you are spending and the public has a right to know what you do with it. It is just the same in the private sector. All public companies are obliged to produce an annual report. They play with shareholders' money and the public sector plays with taxpayers' money. So it's about accountability and governance.

Boasting? Well, why not? The organisation has worked its socks off all year and should be proud of its achievements. The users of the services will want to know, as will the staff. The annual report is the place to flag up new developments. Once again, the staff and the service users will want to know what's coming down the track.

The press will use the annual report as a source of local information, stories and as an archive to refer to during the course of the year. In summary the annual report fulfils several roles:

- a key marketing document
- records the achievements of your organisation
- a statutory document
- a vehicle to state future plans
- a recruitment document – *looks like a nice place to work*
- corporate brochure
- public accountability – not just public relations.

 Exercise

- Consider the key uses of an annual report:

1 a key marketing document
2 records the achievements of your organisation
3 a statutory document
4 a vehicle to state future plans
5 a recruitment document – *looks like a nice place to work*
6 corporate brochure
7 public accountability – not just public relations.

- Arrange them in order of importance and consider how their importance impacts on the weight and space given to each heading in the overall make-up of the document.

TARGET AUDIENCE AND OBJECTIVES

WHO WILL READ IT?

The simple answer is, who do you want to read it? You can send copies to the world and his wife and your granny – but where will it do most good?

There are two obvious audience headings: internal and external.

Internal audiences

Staff, including:

- clinicians at all levels
- administrative and support staff, voluntary groups and 'friends' of the organisation
- staff representatives, such as unions and Royal Colleges.

External audiences

- patients
- general public
- local interest groups
- media
- politicians – national and local
- suppliers
- other healthcare organisations, such as local trusts, health authorities, other commissioners and GPs
- potential new staff – included in a recruitment pack.

OBJECTIVES

What messages do you want to send out? Plan the report like a book. It must have a beginning, a middle and an end. (*Unlike this book – Ed*)

- achievements and developments of the past year
- future plans
- reasons behind strategic decisions.

MAKE IT INTERESTING – HAVE A THEME

Using a theme, running continuously through the report, adds interest and suggests a use for pictures and graphics. Try and make the theme fit the organisation. Here are some examples:

- excellence
- day in the life of . . .
- people – patients and staff.

 Exercise

Make a list of five potential themes that could be sustained throughout an annual report. Try and link them with a communications strategy and demonstrate how they would reinforce important messages.

1   Developing people
2
3
4
5

READABILITY

How many national newspapers are there? No, we don't know either! (*Is there anything you two do know? – Ed*) The important thing is, there is more than one. They range from the *Daily Star* to the *Financial Times*. They each have their target audience and each will have its own approach. In your organisation, there will be folk who read *The Times* and folk who read the *Daily Mirror*.

How do you write an annual report that will be acceptable and readable for them all? They are all your target audience and they will be very different. Different backgrounds, educational achievement, vocabulary . . .

Not easy, eh? The trick is to aim at a middle-of-the-road style that is not patronising and is not so technical it makes your eyes water. Avoid jargon, abbreviations and overlong paragraphs. Pictures tell a story much better than words, so make sure you use 'em, but only the best please.

Think you are writing the report for a relative who knows nothing about the organisation and normally reads the *Daily Express* and you might be right!

THE NITTY GRITTY

PLANNING AND PREPARATION

No one plans to fail, they just fail to plan . . .

The trick is to start where you'll finish. When has the finished report got to land on someone's desk? Once you have the finish date in mind you can work backwards, to where you are now and commit suicide because there isn't enough time left to get the job done! In the NHS world, just like its parallel universe the private sector, the date of the Annual General Meeting will dictate everything.

WHAT HAVE YOU GOT TO DO?

Here's an outline of the key steps along the way.

1   Plan the content and develop the budget – get an idea what the final version contains, how many to print and how much you want to pay for it. The budget will have a big bearing on the number of pages and the choice of full colour, spot colour or black and white.

Done it!

2   Tender process – if you are not gong to do the job 'in-house', bear in mind the length of time it might take to set up a competitive tendering process to find the right company to do it for you. You'll need to:
3   Prepare a short list.

4   Spend time in meetings with bidders to brief them and
    see their work through the process – how's your diary
    and does it fit?

5   Appoint successful bidder.

6   Consider design concepts, try them out with
    colleagues, maybe even the Board.

7   Copy writing – this is press-guru-speak for 'words'.
    Believe it or not, copy writing is a profession in itself.
    The right words, for the right people at the right time.
    Who's going to write the words for your annual
    report? Can you do it yourself, is there someone in
    the organisation that can do it, or is it a job for a
    professional? If you plan to have different parts of the
    report written by different people, bear in mind that
    everyone has a different writing style and it may be
    necessary to edit some of the contributions to keep
    them in line with the theme and general approach. If
    you choose a chatty, open style, a contribution from a
    colleague written like a thesis will have to be tweaked!
    Writing the annual report is not like writing a report, a
    novel or a letter to your Mum!

8   Photography. Good-quality pictures – the more the
    merrier. Next question: colour or black and white?
    You should have sorted this out at the concept stage.
    Who's going to take them?

9   First draft – approval, from whom, will they be
    available to fit into your timescales? How long will
    they take?

10 Second draft – approval, from whom, will they be
    available to fit into your timescales? How long will
    they take? Repetitive, ain't it!

11 Financial data – this stuff always takes longer than
    anything else. You could rewrite *War and Peace* in the
    time it takes the average finance department to tart
    about with the numbers. They have all sorts of
    problems with target rates of returns, auditors,
    reconciliations and general junk and dirty words too
    nasty to be repeated here. Just find out, early, how
    long it will take and mentally double it! Bear in mind
    they must get the accounts signed off for the annual

general meeting and that might help you with the planning.

12   Print and delivery. Printers are put on this earth to drive a saint to distraction! Printers are always late and always work to deadlines that are hairlines. Now, if your other half is a printer and you are outraged with this foul calumny that we have pronounced on a fine profession that has its routes in the inspiration of William Caxton – we're very sorry. But it's true . . . So, leave plenty of time for the ink to dry, so to speak!

13   Despatch prior to AGM, at the AGM or after the AGM? Good question, here's a tricky bit. The annual accounts are signed off and approved at the AGM. So, distributing in advance of the AGM is technically dicey. But, you really need to allow a week before the AGM for the full accounts to be distributed to the great and the good. The rest is up to you!

14   Print run? This is printer-guru-speak for how many copies do you want printed? Well, here's a few neat questions to help you arrive at the answer:
   –   Find out how many copies you had printed last year.
   –   Did you use them all?
   –   How accessible are you going to make the report? Who do you plan to have copies? All of the staff? Every service user? The wider community you serve?
   –   Every supplier?
   –   Are you going to include it in your recruitment pack?
   –   Did anyone get left off last year's list and you **must** include them this time around?

WHO'S GONNA DO ALL THIS GOOD STUFF?

Tricky question this! There is only one captain on a ship and there should be only one person in charge of producing the annual report. They may include teams of colleagues for input and they may have to get their work signed of by the Board but there is only one boss. Not joint responsibility, not job-share, just one person to take all the credit (or blame). You cannot write an annual report by committee. Got that! (*By heck we feel better for getting that off our chests!*)

Timetable?

Once you have the timetable sorted out, base it on the check list above, make a big chart and pin it to the wall – and stick to it! No, not the wall, the timetable. Leave slack in the schedule to allow for colleagues to let you down, go sick, have a holiday (bank on the finance director and CEO both being away at the most critical time) and someone to throw a wobbler. The AGM will not wait – you have to deliver this on time! That's why we are fanatical about one person having the job – no interfaces to trip you up!

What goes in?

In consultant-guru-speak: 'The Brief'. Here's the best advice we have on the subject:

> The better the brief – the better the report

Where can you look for inspiration ?

Here are some ideas.

Will the contributions come from individuals or groups? If there is a group involved, get them to brainstorm ideas. Encourage them to be free-think-ing and write all the ideas on a flip

 **Hazard Warning**
Be clear about the budget and stick to it. Budget over-runners are a bore to work with . . .

chart. No matter how daft the ideas, don't reject them or make the participants feel foolish. Very often a daft idea will lead to another and better idea. List the ideas and then discuss them one by one. Get everyone's agreement and cross out the ideas that cannot be used and develop the ones that can. This approach encourages a sense of participation and ownership.

Ask people who had a copy of last year's report what they would like to see changed, added or left out.

Look at past examples: did they work, can they be improved on?

Get some annual reports from other organisations outside your field. How do they handle it, can you learn anything, or develop an idea for use in your annual report?

Don't forget the obvious stuff, like: background to the organisation and testimonials from satisfied users!

Here are some issues you must decide on

• Internal or external copywriters?

You could have a mixture of the two? It is quite a nice idea to ask users or staff to write a piece from their perspective. You can avoid conflicts of copy-writing style by making it clear that it is written by a member of staff. This can be reinforced, visually, by printing the words on the page, inset, in a box–like this is...

• Internal or external photographers?

A professional photographer will give you high-quality pictures taken on a large format negative that will reproduce well. They may even use a digital camera for the job. Alternatively, you could give a few members of staff one of those cheap disposable cameras each, and turn them loose on the organisation. This works well with a 'day-in-the-life-of' theme. The pics won't be the finest quality but by reproducing them on the same page – perhaps set at an angle or with fake album clips at each corner – the quality issue goes away. The finished result gives an intimate 'look behind the curtains' feel.

⊛ Hazard Warning

Be double, triple and quadruple sure you get the permission of everyone whose picture appears in the report. This is particularly important for patients in the NHS. You must be able to demonstrate they gave *informed* consent. The permission of their caseworker or nurse may not be enough on its own.

• When choosing a photographer, ask around for recommendations and check their portfolios.
• Put the brief in writing. Explain exactly what you want them to do.
• Where possible, accompany the photographer to make sure they don't take a pic of the wrong thing or have a funny five minutes and want to become the next David Bailey, at your expense.

- Aim to get all shots done in a day – that saves money. Make sure there are no delays in the shoot that are attributable to your organisation. Plan well ahead. If necessary, have a dry run to make sure you can get from one side of the town to the other and take 57 photographs all in one day.
- Copyright – who will own the negatives? Ooh, tricky this. Many photographers will try and hang on to the copyright – if they do, find another photographer. Hang on to the ownership of the negatives wherever possible.
- Get an all-in price that includes time, materials, contact sheets and a fixed number of prints.
- If you plan to use medical illustrations or pictures of spanking new medical kit, try a picture library or a pharmaceutical company for illustrations and the manufacturers of the kit for a pic of their whizzo-machine.
- Collect photographs throughout the year and build up a library – great for a 'year-in-the-life' theme.

> ☞ Ask to see a contact sheet of the photographs before letting the photographer make enlargements of the day's work. They may say it is easier to judge the picture quality if the prints are bigger. Have none of it!
>
> You have two choices: reach for your wallet, or reach for a magnifying glass!

PRINT

Monochrome, two colour, or more? Full colour costs, and black and white costs, too. But the difference is obtain down. Get loadsa quotes and let the printer know you're comparing prices. Difference in paper quality make for the biggest price variation. Magazine glossy or free-sheet woolly paper? Can you use a cheaper, less glossy paper as part of the concept. Cheap doesn't have to look cheap. Sometimes cheap can say 'cool'. Be sure about the print run. Extra runs for more copies are budget busters. The binding of the report is another area to explore in the hunt to save money. Stitched spines cost more that stapled and glueing is usually more expensive than tying the report up in pink ribbon!

BUYING PRINT?

Unless you are experienced, it is sometimes better to go for an all-in package with an agency, this is called *design and print*. It means they quote you for doing the design and delivering the printed material. However, this often means the print will be marked-up to reflect the amount of time the agency spend on the job and there is always the hidden element of a 'kick-back' from the printer to the agency. The value of the 'kick-back' has got to go on someone's bill. It is a question of time and money – yours. Which is more valuable?

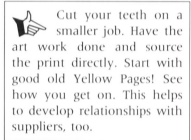 Cut your teeth on a smaller job. Have the art work done and source the print directly. Start with good old Yellow Pages! See how you get on. This helps to develop relationships with suppliers, too.

PRINT AND COLOUR

- One-colour, usually black – this is the cheapest.
- Two-colour, usually black and one other colour, but could be two non-black colours. Remember, creative designs work well in two colours and can look as good as four colour.
- Three-colour, more pricey. In fact it is usually the same price as four-colour. But, it seldom looks expensive. Somehow, three-colour never looks like value for money.
- Four-colour. This is expensive and is wasted without a quality print job and good design.

 Two TIPS for the price of one
1 Spend extra on design rather than four-colour printing.
2 Spend extra on 'heavier paper' for the cover rather than four-colour printing.

GETTING THE BRIEF RIGHT

Use the brief-writing process to identify where help is needed. The brief should outline cost and the importance of documents. There is a direct relationship between cost and importance

Use the 'brief' to create processes to involve others and gain a sense of internal 'ownership' from colleagues. Ask for feedback, for thoughts and ideas. Encourage them to be creative – use brainstorming to develop innovative thinking.

SPONSORSHIP

The cost of producing a really first-class report can be made more manage-able by working with a private sector partner – the third way! It used to be called sponsorship but times have moved on!

Why should a company be bothered with sponsorship? For many, it is being seen to be connected with the community. There is an element of altruism but it is mainly about image and the fact that some sponsorship is a tax-deductible business expense. (*Oh, so cynical – Ed*) The truth is, a sponsor cannot really expect a flood of business as a result of sponsoring your annual report. Just bear in mind you get '*owt for nowt*' in this world and be certain that any relationship with a sponsor sits comfortably with your corporate governance responsibilities.

 Hazard Warning

Be sure to pay special attention to the needs of the visually impaired and ethnic communities where English is not the first language. You may need to plan for translation into, perhaps, more than one language.

How will you integrate the languages in the design without making them appear as a suffix, stuck at the back? Translations into Braille, or transition onto audio tape, ake time. Allow for i in the timetable e sure to bring all of the editions o the document out o the same day. / ything else is discourteous and looks like an after thought.

How do you go about it?

Once the decision has been made to accept or seek a sponsor (a d this is usually a decision for the Board), the next step s to create a bri Decide what you want from a sponsor and what you can give a sponsor in return. Be clear what the sponsor will get for the money.

- Look locally for sponsors. Look among your suppliers and look among the rela-tives of staff! Diamonds are generally found beneath the soles of you feet!
- Was there a sponsor last year? Will they do it again?
- Look at specific industries or companies with whom you wish to collaborate in

 Hazard Warning
If you are in doubt about it being right and the sponsor is keen – best to say 'No Thanks'!

the future. Be careful about conflicts of interest or being seen to favour one prospective supplier over another.

- There are a number of agencies who specialise in sponsorship – can they help?
- Don't let sponsorship dominate the report – subtly is best.

21 TIPS FOR A TOP REPORT

1   Encourage feedback from all your audiences – include a tear-out section for comments.

Yup! Gotcha!

2   Collect patient comments via patient surveys and include them to give the report a human face.
3   Use the report to advertise how to make complaints.
4   Use newspaper cuttings to highlight your achievements.
5   Include good practice and practical tips on self-help.
6   Include important contact data such as names, telephone numbers, maps, a guide around the hospital.
7   Avoid jargon – enter and try and win the Plain English Award.
8   Short simple sentences – be aware of the diversity of the readership.
9   Use bold, clear typefaces, in size 10- to 12-point.
10 Think about translations, audio tapes, Braille versions.
11 Fewer pages are more likely to be read.
12 Be sure to get value for money in buying print and design.
13 Two-colour printing can often work as well as four.
14 Look at the choice of paper stock.
15 Make a report look more substantial by using a heavier stock for outside cover and lighter inside.

16   Can medical illustration help?

17   Use staff and public competitions for illus-
     trations, drawings, photographs and artwork.

18   Use the 'day-in-the-life-of' approach for
     photography.

19   Revisit the distribution list – is everyone
     that should be getting it, getting it? If they
     haven't got it, you haven't published it! Are
     you producing too many?

20   Sponsorship: choose the right partner – and
     ask what are they getting out of it?

21   Collect ideas for copy throughout the year.

AND NOW FOR SOMETHING COMPLETELY DIFFERENT . . .

Can you be innovative? Most newspapers and magazines are published on
the Internet. What about your report? What, not got a web site? Oh dear!
Best go and find a job with a progressive company making gas lamps. You've
put all this work in, you must want loadsa people to see what a stunning job
you've done! Here are some more ideas to help get the message across to a
bigger audience.

- Link with local newspapers – get them to publish a straight copy of
  your report as a supplement, or talk to them about including a version
  of the report as an insert in the paper. This is all good community
  publishing stuff – they like all that!
- CD look-alike? Use a traditional CD cover as the packaging to contain
  your annual report – it will command attention and ensure that it gets
  looked at.
- Better still, put the report on to a CD-ROM. You can get a blank CD
  printed for a few pence – much less than you think. Then you can
  include video footage and links to your web site. The software to
  load is simple to use and not expensive. Very exciting and sexy,
  dontchafink?
- Wall calendar: include a calendar format for your report and be front of
  mind for the whole year. And it's a great place to sell advertising. Or a
  desk calendar or desk diary.

FINAL, FINAL, FINAL CHECKLIST   *Yup!*

- Know your audience

- Know your objectives

- Have easily readable text

- Use short and simple sentences

- Good design is better than four-colour printing

- Consider a theme – key messages to run through the report

- Think about print runs, distribution

- Use media and patients' comments

- Spend money on external skills to strengthen your own team

- Don't go for the cheapest quote

- Consider: time, quality and budget money

- Plan carefully and stick to your timetable

FINALLY

Finally, finally, finally, finally finally, finally, finally finally, finally, finally finally, finally, finally finally, finally, finally finally, finally, finally finally, finally, finally finally, finally, finally . . .

Make sure you have a communications strategy to launch your report. Bet you nearly forgot that!

No good doing all that hard work if you aren't going to mark a successful publication with some carefully planned activity.

REPORT LAUNCHING

Here are a few ideas to start you off, to get you going and on the right track for report launching:

- Send a copy of the summary report to each member of staff with a personal '*thank you*' letter from the boss (that'll make you think about how many you have to print).

- Arrange one-to-one briefings for local media, but don't just talk about what has happened over the last 12 months, use it as an opportunity to point to the exciting plans you have on the horizon.
- Before you sit down with journalists, think of the most difficult questions you are likely to be asked and frame the answers you will give, then try them out on colleagues. (Remember the rules: never tell a lie and never say 'no comment'.)
- Arrange for the boss to address meetings of local special interest groups to present the report and answer their questions.
- Get spreads (*guru-speak for sections*) from your report enlarged and mounted on to display boards and site them where people are likely to see them. Think about places inside the organisation where a lot of people move about and then think about places outside the organisation – such as supermarkets and shops. Mmm, you can only ask and keep asking until someone says: 'Yup, come and do it!'.

CALLING FOR THE CAVALRY

A consultant is someone who can take something you already know and make it sound confusing!

FINDING, RECRUITING AND KEEPING COMMUNICATIONS CONSULTANTS

What do you want to recruit a consultant in communications for? You've got this book, haven't you! Well, we admit, there are still *one or two* good reasons.

Maybe you have an in-tray full of stuff and although you know how to do the job you don't know how to fit it in. Too, busy? Well that's not a bad reason provided you've done a genuine job on time management and prioritised your workload. If you are up against the clock, a relationship with a good consultant, who can be trusted to get on with the job, is a godsend.

Then there is the 'wood-for-the-trees' reason. Sometimes a fresh pair of eyes brings an objectivity and a fresh set of ideas. Perhaps you do have internal skills and they need some support. Recruiting a consultant can be seen as part of a learning exercise and developing people.

And, here is the crunch reason. You've been honest enough to admit communications is a vital part of what needs to be done and you are big enough to confess you don't know enough about it to get it right first time.

Some reasons to get in outside help with communications:

- You want to develop a strategy based on the findings of a communications audit – it's generally more sensible to have a third party do this for you. Staff and your key audiences can speak candidly knowing that their views will be treated in the strictest confidence.

- You have a specific task – like producing the annual report, writing recruitment literature or the in-house newspaper – but no one available with the right skills in-house to steer it through to a successful conclusion.

- Your senior managers need to polish up on their presentation and media skills – an outside consultant can help and not be afraid to tell the chief executive he's rubbish! (In a nice way, of course!) (*Rubbish is still rubbish even if you call it litter – Ed*)

- You are planning some major changes to your organisation and need to put a community relations programme into action to ensure that local views are carefully considered.

WHERE DO YOU FIND A CONSULTANT?

Ask other organisations if they know of, or use, outside help? Look on the last page of an annual report and see if there is n me of a consulta t printed on it.

GET THE RIGHT HORSE FOR THE COURSI

What are you looking for in a consultancy?

It must have experience in the sector you are working in. A communications consultant who does a great job for a car manufacturer may not be the right choice for you if you are not in the automotive business. A public sector specialist is not likely to be of much use to a chain of supermarkets. In fact, the public sector is a very specialised market. The NHS, social services, education – all have very specialised needs. Be sure to go for someone who has worked in that market and your sector.

No doubt you will invite several com-

 If the person who will be looking after you is present and makes a significant input into the presentation, answers all your questions and if they don't know, asks one of the team for help – lock the door, you may have found the last good consultant on earth!

panies to come and pitch for your account. They will turn up with their best team and try to impress you. Ask the question: 'Who is going to be looking after my account?'. If the answer is, *'The person who will be doing your work isn't here'*, show them all the door. If the person who will be looking after you is with the team doing the pitch but doesn't say anything, show them all the door. If the person who will be looking after you is present and makes a significant input into the presentation, answers all your questions and if they don't know, asks one of the team for help, lock the door, you may have found the last good consultant on earth!

Who else have they worked for? Ask them, get a list but don't leave it there. Ring up the firms they are working for and have worked for and ask the question: *'Are they any good?'*

Ask: 'How was it for you daahling?' – that's what you want to know. If the reply is furtive or less than fulsome, there's probably something to hide. Show them the door!

Do they command credibility in the market. Do they sound credible. Do they have a decent address and proper offices? In these days of the virtual company, home working and everyone tooled up to the eyeballs with IT gizmos, an address is not the key determinant it once was.

Do you like them? Can you get on with them? Where do they appear on the rapport-ometer? You don't have to fall in love with them but it is helpful if you like them – they share two senses: your sense of humour and your sense of urgency.

In fact there is something to be said for people who work with low overheads – their fees should be cheaper. It's a balance.

Make an unannounced visit to their trading address and make your own mind up.

GOT 'EM. NOW, GET THE BEST FROM THEM

- Don't overlook in-house staff and remember, your folk will learn from the consultants. So, buy-in the gaps, plug the skill cracks with consultant time.
- Use consultants to add to your to your 'team' – make it more skilful by getting in the right external support. Treat the consultant as 'one of the family'. A good consultant will be happy to work with in-house people and play his or her part.
- Give one in-house person overall responsibility to work with the external consultant, to commission external work and to manage the

external agency. That way you avoid interfaces and the prospect of any lack of clarity in the instructions, and the consultant can never say: 'Freda told me one thing and now you are telling me different'.

- Make sure you know what you want the external consultant to do and be crystal-clear about the brief. Make sure the consultancy knows and understands this.
- Know who will be responsible at the consultancy? Who do you have to connect with if things go wrong, or things go so well you want to ring up and say: 'Well done!'?
- Get a clear handle on the costs. Agree all costs and remember the small print. Look out for extras such as 'disbursements' – when, what, and how much? Look for travel costs and mark-ups.

Beware! This is a trap for the trusting . . .

SOME DOs AND DON'Ts

1   Don't just choose the cheapest.
2   Don't choose based on the quality of the documents or 'visuals' you are shown in the tender documents – ask to see copies of real work, for real clients.
3   Do try and get a feel for the consultancy's overall capabilities. Can they do everything you ask? Are they good at visuals but not so hot on copy writing? Can they do the external stuff but have no track record of working internally, with staff?
4   Do judge the quality of what they do. Judge on accuracy, right first time, following the brief, as well as the image their work creates.
5   Don't put up with a consultancy, however good, that doesn't stick to deadlines and timescales.
6   Do go for experience. This may cut out the attractive start-up agency, keen to please. But, if you are responsible for hiring a firm of consultants and they let you down, you'll be the one to catch it in the neck.
7   Do think carefully about cost. Cheapest isn't always the best and be sure to understand the likely impact of any unexpected extras on the bill.

Got it!

8 Do ask yourself the question: what is more important, a job done quickly, a job done cheaply, or a job done well and to a high quality?

9 Do start with a comprehensive brief and make sure everyone understands it.

10 Do use the brief as basis for discussion with designers and consultancies.

11 Do use the brief to tender – get quotes.

12 Do invest time, be open-minded and try to meet new people with new ideas.

13 Don't be afraid to try a new firm out on a small, introductory project.

14 Don't be afraid to have more than one consultancy working for you. Create a 'stable' of trusted experienced designers and consultancies.

15 Do make sure that the agency/designer understands what you want and can deliver.

HATED THE WORDS AND MUSIC — LOVED THE VIDEO

The best way to stop kids looking at naughty movies is to label them 'educational'!

CAN A VIDEO PLAY A USEFUL PART IN EFFECTIVE COMMUNICATIONS?

A video can have its place in the communications arsenal. It has impact. It will be remembered and can provide an opportunity for staff, patients and other important folk to star. However, you are generally forced into the hands of professional production companies whose ideas of low budget compared to your own are usually poles apart.

 Hazard Warning

Don't be taken for a ride – these days videos do not have to cost a fortune!

Don't get seduced by the 'show biz' nature of the medium. Stay level-headed about it all!

CUTTING THE COST TO SUIT YOUR COAT

- There are ways of getting things on the road without breaking the bank, but you've go to think laterally. A local college or university offering multimedia courses might like to be invited to take on the task. It would be a good way for the students to get practical experience and it could even be regarded as a community project and that makes everyone feel better. Tapping into the creative juices of the students could produce a dazzling production! (*Or a pint of beer – Ed*)

- A video could be a sitter (*sponsorship-guru-speak for sitting target*) for sponsorship – provided your sponsorship partner is chosen carefully (*Sorry, you'll have to go back and read Section 6*) and the benefits are clearly defined for them.

- Look to see if you have any local celebrities who could be persuaded to appear or lend their voice for the commentary. It's good PR for them and it could save you a packet. (*Just like choosing your sponsor partners though, be careful who you approach. We wonder if the rail company Connex is regretting having used Gary Glitter to advertise their young persons rail saver card?*)

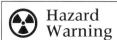 **Hazard Warning**

Be careful in choosing a local celebrity to donate their time to your video production – they might have embarrassing skeletons in the cupboard!

Making a video indoors means you have control over the lighting, sound and weather – it's cheaper!

- Planning a 'shoot' (*more guru-speak, for where and when you make this masterpiece*) carefully will definitely keep the costs down. There is nothing a production company likes better than to be faced with several days on location. You can hear them counting the money! If you have agreed the purpose and the content in advance, you should be in a position to ensure that all the interviewees are in one place at the same time or on adjacent sites that can be reached easily in a single day.

- Get more out of the video by uploading some of the images on to your web site.

DEVELOP A CLEAR BRIEF

If you are going down this route be very clear about what it is you will be using your video for. If you are just doing it because it sounds cool, forget it right now. It may be, for instance, that you are developing a recruitment strategy and have to visit far-away places. A video becomes a great way to show potential employees what your organisation and the local community is all about. Or, maybe you are planning to attend a number of high-profile conferences or exhibitions and need something to get folk on to your stand. A video could be the answer.

VHS tapes are the conventional format that most of us are familiar with, but these days videos can be downloaded on to CDs and these can be played on a bog standard PC or a laptop computer provided they have a sound card. Don't worry, most do.

The 'in-line video' (*video-guru-speak for a continuous production storyline*) is the conventional format – a beginning, middle and end.

However, if you really have money to spend on this or if you can persuade a sponsor to part with some real cash, you can produce a CD ROM version that works just like a web site. This will allow your different audiences to find their own pathway to the parts of your production that are of specific interest to them. Oh, so coooooool!

> In the old days, videos had the distinct disadvantage that once produced you were then stuck with them. Nowadays technology allows for inexpensive editing on the master tape should circumstances change. So, if the CEO who has been used to introduce the show gets the boot just as the videos are delivered, don't worry. Insert the new CEO at the flick of a button. Good news for film makers, bad news for CEOs!

THE DOs AND DON'Ts OF VIDEO MAKING

- Don't think you can't do it because it's too expensive.
- Do be creative – consider using schools, technical colleges and evening class groups to make the video if you can't afford a production company.
- Do consider quality versus money. It is not necessarily the case that the more you spend the better it gets.
- Do think about the storyline. Start by brainstorming with colleagues – what goes in? Get agreement and win ownership. Plan the order.
- A production company will script it for you, but make sure you see storyboards and the script before it goes too far.
- Do get as much done in one place as possible.
- Don't let the video makers out of your sight for one minute. Every minute costs you money and the wrong pictures of the wrong thing means a row and more costs.
- Do make sure the people you want in the video are prepared to take part.
- Make sure you get to see rough cuts to ensure that no gaffs get through to the final stage.

- Don't forget consent issues.
- Don't use a production agency unless you have seen other examples of what they've done.
- Do talk to their customers – how was it for them?
- Don't sign a contract until you know what the costs are.
- Don't get caught by having to pay loadsamoney for copies.
- Do get a handle on copyright issues – like who owns it when it is finished (it should be you).
- Do be clear about the use you intend to put the video to. Will a 'one-video-fits-all' product suit every occasion?

ADVERTISING — SOMETHING ELSE IN YOUR IN-TRAY

The freedom of the press in Britain is to print as much of the proprietor's prejudices as the advertisers don't object to.

The difference between advertising and editorial is a matter of control (*and money – Ed!*). You control, within reason, the paid for message contained within the borders of a display advertisement. The control of what appears elsewhere is in the gift of the editor.

 **Hazard Warning**

The Advertising Standards Authority will want to ensure that your advertisement is truthful, honest and does not mislead.

However, there are occasions when the editor may choose to exercise their right to refuse to publish your advertisement.

The 'within reason' means that your message must conform to the strict rules of the Advertising Standards Authority and be truthful, honest and not mislead.

An advertisement, whether it appears in print or is broadcast, is an opportunity to put over a controlled message about your organisation. So make the most it!

WHAT ARE THE RULES?

Remember the lessons about deadlines for editorial? These apply equally to advertising. In some instances the lead times can be even longer. Artwork may need to be made up and proofs be approved. So the first message is: leave yourself plenty of time and plan well ahead. Know how long before a publication goes to press that your advertisement needs to be on the desk of someone at the newspaper, magazine, or radio or TV station.

WATCH OUT FOR THE TECHNICAL BITS

If it is a printed publication, find out whether it requires artwork in the form of:

- positive or negative film
- a PMT (*No, it's not what you're thinking. It means a photomechanical transfer. See, talking like an adver-guru already!*)
- on disk and in what format (most printers use a piece of software called Quark Xpress. It is almost beyond belief, though true, that something produced in Word will not be acceptable; it has to go through a conversion process. Yup, we know what you're thinking and this time you're probably right – printers are an awkward bunch! However, basic versions of Quark are not expensive and are easy to use – so you know the answer and what to ask Santa to pop into your stocking)
- whether you can e-mail your copy for the advert to them, to give yourself a bit more time.

> Printers like to make the technical bits as difficult as possible, so it might be time to think about using an ad agency to do all this for you. However, remember, no one does anything for nothing. If you are placing the odd advert here or there, expect an agency to give you a bill. So, hunt through this book and find the section on hiring a consultant – all that good stuff applies here, too. However, if you are placing loadsa-adverts, the agency may be happy with the commission they can get from the paper/mag/TV/radio station for placing your advert in the media.

WHEN TO ADVERTISE — AND WHAT?

Adverts, extolling the virtue of a product or service are the preserve of the Henriettas and Henrys in the marketing department. Collectively known as the 'Hernias'. Let them get on with that.

The communications gurus expect to deal with so-called corporate advertising.

This could include:

- Advertising a public meeting. (*Read all about them in the free supplement at the back.*)
- Recruitment. The Gladys's and the George's, collectively known as the 'Glades' in the personnel department or human resources department (*sometimes know as the Human Remains Department*) may ask you to help sort out their recruitment advertising.
- Publicising an achievement. Usually the boss's office gets on the phone and says the CEO is at an awards dinner tonight. He's picking up an award for the best organisation in the Galaxy and wants to have an advert in the journals, blowing our bugle, tomorrow. The answer is likely to be: we didn't get to be an award-winning company by not understanding copy deadlines; go away and come back when you live in the real world; or send a copy of this book to the tenth floor and earmark this section. Any of these answers is likely to be career-limiting – so demonstrate what a star communication guru you are and just do it!

This is all the kind of stuff for which you could be buying space or air time.

WHAT GOES IN

- Think about what you want to say. In guru-speak, the message you wish to convey. The style of ad' says a lot about your organisation. Should you be straight-laced or is there room for some humour? Can you be slightly zany or is formal the order of the day? You can communicate excitement, happiness, seriousness, all through the copy and layout of an advert.
- The corporate identity of the organisation – designer-guru speak for use of logos and typefaces. Does your organisation have a logo? What does it say? Logos are best when they are a strong, single image that can be reproduced in a range of sizes – from posters to the bottom of a business card. So, nothing intricate or fussy. They should also look as good in black and white as they do in colour. So, don't make the success of the image depend on colour. Getting the logo right is a tricky business.
- Who will do the make-up? (*guru-speak for designing the advert.*) Sometimes a newspaper will include the cost of simple artwork in the

price of the advert. Similarly, some radio and TV stations have package deals for first-time advertisers. Check if it's included in the price.

- The distribution (*in advert-guru-speak, sometimes referred to as the 'reach' of the message. That means who will hear it or see it*).
- The shelf life of the medium. Newspapers are for a day, magazines a month, TV and radio 30 seconds. (*Unless the magazines are in a doctor's surgery, in which case they seem to last from 1968 – Ed.*)
- The size of the ad and where it will appear in a publication. Ad space is like property. Only three things matter – position, position, position. Size costs money. Consider a size versus frequency trade-off.
- If you are choosing to use local radio or television, what time of day and how frequently will your ad' be aired? When are your target market most likely to be listening. In the car, to and from work, lunchtime, during the morning or late at night? No good advertising for night security staff at 11 am – they'll all be in bed!
- Above all, **how much will it cost** and can you get a discount? Publications and electronic media will often offer discounts at the last moment, when a salesman needs to fill a slot in order to meet a revenue target – be bold and ask!

 Exercise

- From a newspaper, clip three ads from competing companies, but for the same products. Say computers, or holidays, etc.

- Identify the similarities and the differences. Which ad works best? Why? If there are few differences is it because the ads are all aimed at a similar market and well-targeted, or is it just copy-cat lack of imagination?

- Now do the same exercise with ads from the jobs pages. Pick three ads from the same employment sector. How do the companies present themselves? What are the differences? Do they change their ads to fit in with the target employee, or are they all the same?

The really smart firms will change their approach to fit their target yet, at the same time, retain their branding and image. Good examples of this are Virgin and Nike.

Even though you are dealing with corporate advertising (that is non-product or service advertising), you can still use the lessons of branding to develop your organisation's image.

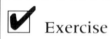 **Exercise**

- Design an ad for your organisation encouraging women, in the 30–45 age bracket, with the skills you need, to return to the workplace, with you.

- Consider the content:
  - opportunities
  - retraining
  - flexible, family friendly hours
  -
  -
  - *what else?*

- Consider where the ad (press or magazines) might be placed:
  - local press
  - national
  - journals
  - radio or TV
  -
  -
  - *what else?*

- List the other factors to take into account:
  - style of copy
  - layout
  - size
  - frequency
  -
  -
  - *what else?*

FREE COLOUR SUPPLEMENT!

This book is black and white and read all over . . .

PUBLIC MEETINGS

'Audience with me all the way . . . managed to shake them off at the station!'

The communications opportunity . . .

WHAT GOES ON BEHIND THE GREEN DOOR?

When you think about it, health is pretty important to us all. One way or another, the NHS and associated services will play a part in our lives and the lives and wellbeing of all of our families and friends.

How decisions are made and the consequences of them could be vital to us. BUT and it is a very BIG BUT, none of us get a chance to vote for the people who make the decisions about our healthcare. Every five years we get the chance to chuck one lot out of Westminster and let another lot in. In between times, decisions about rationing healthcare, the configuration of services, and who gets what and where, are left to an unelected group of managers and clinicians who do the best they can with what they've got. Unless we want to dig up the democratic process and plant something new, we've got to try and make the present system a bit more accountable. The best we can do is to open up the process so that, at the very least, we can let the public watch the decisions being made. They may not agree, but they can't say they haven't had the chance to see how decisions are arrived at.

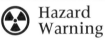 New legislation (The Public Bodies (Admission to Meetings) (National Health Service Trusts) Order 1997: No 2763) came into effect on 6 February 1998, and means that NHS Trusts and PCGs must hold their meetings in public.

☢ Hazard Warning

So who's going to handle all this? What's the betting it ends up in the tray marked '**You**' – the communications guru!

HERE'S HOW IT ALL WORKS

- First, this is not a cosmetic exercise, open board meetings must mean the public should be able to observe the decision making process.
- It is not enough to make it just a spectator sport, the public must be able to understand the internal arguments, tensions and restrictions which lead to a decision.
- So, no fixing up the decisions in advance.

☢ Hazard Warning

Notice of any PCG and Trust meeting, open to the public, must be given at least three days in advance. The time and place of the meeting must be published so that newspapers are able to report the meeting's decisions. You must provide them with the agenda and appropriate papers. Under normal deadlines they will need a week's notice of meetings.

So, you've got to do it: how to do it well is the question.

Tips for making public meetings a communications opportunity

- Make the public feel welcome. Make sure the seats are comfortable and they can all see and hear what is going on and the venue is somewhere easy for them to get to. Check that there is good public transport and easy parking. Give someone the specific task of welcoming the public, pointing out where the loos are, directing them to where they can sit. Appoint a friendly meeter and greeter.
- Make sure whoever chairs the meeting makes some encouraging introductory remarks. If there are a lot of people there, because there is a controversial item on the agenda, try: *'Thank you all for coming. I know there will be some issues that are of great concern to many of you – as they are to us. I'm pleased to see so many of you have taken the trouble to come and see how tough it can be sometimes to make finely balanced and difficult decisions. I'm pleased you will be able to witness the fact we do our best to listen to the facts and make a decision on our best judgement. Unfortunately we do not have the Wisdom of Solomon, but we try and use the common sense and experience that we all have. Some of you will be pleased with what we decide, others, perhaps not. We can only do our best for you.'*

⚛ **Hazard Warning**

The tone of introductory remarks can set the tone for the whole meeting. Think, in advance, about what to say.

Say it and mean it. Preparation is the key – don't try and do it off the cuff.

- If it is routine and a man and his dog have turned up, make them feel special: *'Thank you so much for turning out. We admire your dedication! I hope, by the time of the next meeting you will have been able to persuade a neighbour, relative or friend that it is worth their time to come with you'*. And, give the dog a biscuit!
- Introduce the members of the board and explain their speciality. *'Dr So and So, from the Down-Town Practice; Mary Smith from Social Services; Mrs Bloggs the health authority nominee'* – and so on. It helps the public understand where the members are coming from.
- Provide nameplates for board members to remind the public who the members are.

- Give the public copies of the agenda and papers being discussed.
- Consider holding a press briefing before the meeting to be sure the media understands the issues to be discussed.
- Make sure the seating is arranged in such a way that the public can follow the discussion. For example, this could mean seating the board in a horseshoe arrangement facing out, towards the public and press.
- If slides or overheads are used, make sure the public can see the screen.
- Can you provide an audio loop? They can be hired for the meeting. You should do it, particularly if elderly people who may have hearing difficulties are likely to attend. You may even need to consider someone who can interpret using sign language.
- What's disabled access like – token ramps or the real thing? Don't get caught out on this one; ask local disability representation groups to give you advice.
- Can you provide a crèche facility?
- Are there language issues? Think about translations of the printed word and perhaps translation of issues of particular interest and concern to an ethnic group.
- Have the staff been told about the meeting – make them feel welcome, too.
- What about switching the venue to make it easier for people to get to. Rotate the venues.
- If specific items for discussion are likely to be of interest to specific groups, consider holding the meeting at an appropriate venue. Young people issues in a school. For mum's and toddlers; try the local supermarket; the elderly, how about a day centre. Meetings can move, you know, it's just your brains we want, not your address!

OK, SO YOU'VE GOT THEM THERE, NOW WHAT?

Unless decisions are seen to be made openly, there is no point having meetings in public. The whole idea is to let people see how its all done and feel part of the process and to encourage public.

- Policy options and ideas should be brought before the Board for genuine debate and decision without rehearsal or prior agreement on the outcome.
- Arguments for and against proposals should be aired in public.
- Make the Community Health Council your ally, involve them, too.

Timing of meetings is important

Consider the possibility of some meetings being held outside normal working hours to allow making it easier for the general public to attend.

 Within the terms of the legislation, members of the public and press do not have a right to speak at meetings.

However, there is nothing to stop the chair inviting contributions and questions. Your Board may wish to make time in the agenda, at the beginning or end of meetings, when questions can be taken.

Or, what about asking the public to submit written questions for you to answer?

When can you close the doors?

This is technical stuff, so pay attention! The Public Bodies (Admission to Meetings) 1960 Act includes provision for the discussion of confidential business in private sessions. Under the terms of the Act, a board may resolve to 'exclude the public from a meeting (whether during the whole or part of the proceedings) whenever publicity would be prejudicial to the public interest by reason of the confidential nature of the business to be transacted or for other special reasons stated in the resolution . . .'. So now you know!

 **Hazard Warning**

Don't abuse the powers or you will bring the wrath of the Secretary of State down upon you! Nasty!

Limit closed sessions to:

- where real harm to individuals may result – this might include discussion about particular members of staff for disciplinary or other reasons, or relate to independent reviews on complaints

- a discussion of financial issues might be prejudicial to competitive tendering or similar issues.

The resolution should be taken in public, and recorded in the minutes. It should state in broad terms (which do not breach the confidentiality of the subject matter) the nature of the business to be discussed.

It should not be used however as a means of sparing board members from public criticism or proper public scrutiny.

CHC representatives and other appropriate individuals may attend closed board meetings at the board's discretion.

WHAT ABOUT SUBCOMMITTEES?

Smart question!

The provisions of the Act do not relate to subcommittees of the main board unless all board members are members of the subcommittee. It is recognised that the subject matter of audit and remuneration committees, as well as committees looking at issues such as complaints and appointments, will, in any event, generally be of a confidential nature.

However, no cheating! The establishment of subcommittees should not be used as a means of diverting business which is properly a matter for the full board or to avoid issues being addressed in public. Furthermore, none of this precludes an invitation to the public to attend meetings of any subcommittee.

Primary care groups, which have devolved decision-making powers on commissioning, are a special type of health authority subcommittee and the public should have access to its meetings. The law will be tweaked to sort out this anomaly. In the meantime you should behave like the big boys do and meet in public.

IF YOU GET IT WRONG?

Complaints from the public about access to board meetings or the provision of information about them or their proceedings should be dealt with in the same way as complaints under the Code of Openness in the NHS. That means, complaints should be made, in the first instance, to the senior officer, accountable to the Chief Executive, who has responsibility for the Code.

Dissatisfied complainants should take their complaints directly to the Chief Executive of the NHS body involved, who will provide them with information about how to take their complaint further to the Health Service Ombudsman if they remain dissatisfied. The Ombudsman publishes two reports a year with his findings. These can then come under the scrutiny of the Parliamentary Health Select Committee, with

the guilty parties called to account in a Starr Chamber-like hearing –
serious stuff!

HOW GOOD WAS IT?

It's simple enough to find out. Ask. Have an exit questionnaire at the
meeting, a feedback form, do an exit survey . . . Ask!

- Was the venue easy to get to?
- Was the parking OK?
- Do you have special needs – what are they/were they met?
- Could you hear?
- Could you see?
- Did you understand it all?
- Did you ask a question?
- Are you satisfied with the answer?
- What would you like us to know/tell us?
- Would you like a copy of our annual report?
- Will you come next time?
- Where did you hear about the meeting?

 Some folk are more inclined to tick a box than write answers to questions. So, design a form that gives people options to choose from.

And don't forget to say *Thank You!*

⊛ Hazard Warning

Please note that http web site addresses can, and do, change at short
notice – so, if you come across changes to any of the addresses given in
this book, or indeed find other sites of relevant interest, do let us know.
Contact Roy via his own web site:

http://www.roylilley.co.uk

INDEX